ROUGH DIAMONDS

ROUGH DIAMONDS

THE FOUR TRAITS
OF SUCCESSFUL BREAKOUT
FIRMS IN BRIC COUNTRIES

Seung Ho Park
Nan Zhou
Gerardo R. Ungson

JB JOSSEY-BASS™
A Wiley Brand

Cover design by Adrian Morgan
Cover image: Copyright © Shutterstock
Published by Jossey-Bass
A Wiley Brand
One Montgomery Street, Suite 1200, San Francisco, CA
94104-4594—www.josseybass.com

Jossey-Bass books and products are available through most bookstores. To contact Jossey-Bass directly call our Customer Care Department within the U.S. at 800-956-7739, outside the U.S. at 317-572-3986, or fax 317-572-4002.

Wiley also publishes its books in a variety of electronic formats and by print-on-demand. Some material included with standard print versions of this book may not be included in e-books or in print-on-demand. If the version of this book that you purchased references media such as CD or DVD that was not included in your purchase, you may download this material at http://booksupport.wiley.com. For more information about Wiley products, visit www.wiley.com.

Library of Congress Cataloging-in-Publication Data
Park, Seung Ho, 1960–
    Rough diamonds: the four traits of successful breakout firms in BRIC countries / by Seung Ho Park, Nan Zhou, Gerardo R. Ungson.—First edition.
        pages cm
    Includes bibliographical references and index.
    ISBN 978-1-118-58926-7 (cloth); ISBN 978-1-118-58922-9 (ebk.);
ISBN 978-1-118-58951-9 (ebk.); ISBN 978-1-118-58955-7 (ebk.)
    1. Industrial management—Developing countries. 2. Industries—Developing countries. 3. Industrial policy—Developing countries. 4. Economic development—Developing countries. I. Zhou, Nan, 1982– II. Ungson, Gerardo R. III. Title.
    HD70.D44P37 2013
    658.4′06—dc23

                                                                    2012048752

Printed in the United States of America
FIRST EDITION
HB Printing   10 9 8 7 6 5 4 3 2 1

Contents

Foreword

For those few skeptics who still wondered how far-reaching an impact the world's developing markets will have on the global economy, the recent recession provided a pretty compelling answer. Even as the advanced markets in North America and Europe stumbled into recession from 2007 to 2009, and in some cases beyond, emerging markets continued to post significantly higher growth rates—collectively, as much as 5 percentage points higher.

By now, the primary debate about the potential of developing economies has shifted from the discussion of whether they will continue expanding to discussions about how fast they will grow and for how long they can sustain these remarkable rates. The world's top multinationals have already recognized the key role that developing markets will play in their futures. Brazil, Russia, India, and China (BRIC) have become the world's most sought-after markets, drawing new companies and investments with a combination of sizable populations, rising incomes, developing market institutions, and emerging middle classes. For businesses, sustained growth in these BRIC markets is a foregone conclusion, a given that has led many to look for even newer growth markets in Africa, the Middle East, and South America and across much of Asia.

No doubt multinationals from around the world will continue to play a critical role in the ongoing progression of the BRICs and other emerging economies. After all, the countries that have cut themselves off from the global economy and outside investments have seen their economies suffer for it. Yet no national economy can thrive on outside investment alone. Inevitably only the continued rise of domestic companies, reliable market institutions, and a combination of domestic and international trade can sustain the development of these key emerging economies.

The developing BRIC economies can boast a growing roster of home-grown champions that are leading the way. The likes of Tata (India), Gazprom (Russia), Sinopec (China), and Petrobras (Brazil) have long established themselves as globally recognized brands. They challenge even the greatest of multinationals in terms of expertise, innovation, and leadership in their industries. They've set the standard for business in emerging markets. They are the vanguard.

They are not, however, the ticket to broader economic development, at least not on their own. The true power that is fueling genuinely sustainable growth in these markets is coming from the large but often overlooked tier of successful companies and brands that, while not yet household names worldwide, have posted long-term growth rates far higher than those of most of their counterparts in both emerging and developed economies. These companies, including the rough diamonds identified in this book, provide the supporting foundation of domestic growth that necessarily underpins the ongoing development of a broader marketplace and increasingly robust economy in their home countries.

Yet their impact ripples well beyond the people they employ, the products they develop, and the production they contribute to the national and global economies. These companies raise the bar for both public and private entities. Their business demands force governments and regulatory agencies to establish a framework that sustains and enhances development. Their innovation forces staid old companies to raise their game if they want to remain competitive. Their ever-increasing quality raises both the expectations and the capabilities of their customers. And in many cases, their progressive management and world-class leadership vastly improve workplace standards and worker productivity across entire industries.

This sort of fundamental development, if it is to take a solid foothold in emerging economies, must come from within. It has to grow organically, so it can accommodate the idiosyncrasies of each individual country—its history, culture, and political ecosystem. No doubt the global economy has helped establish market institutions and standards of commerce that benefit businesses in any participating nation. Yet within each nation and each domestic market, this tier of long-term growth companies will provide the true foundation for a sustainable economic development.

Perhaps the only guarantee for these emerging economies is that global and domestic forces will arise to challenge their growth. Recessions will occur. Market institutions will stumble. Regulations will fail. And businesses will rise and fall. It's human nature and it's the fundamental nature of human economies.

But the stronger the foundation of companies with established business models and long-term growth histories is, the better these developing economies will weather the storms and the more they will thrive in the good times.

John Quelch
Harvard Business School

Preface

Across from the Beijing offices of the SKOLKOVO Business School–Ernst & Young Institute for Emerging Market Studies (IEMS) is Olympic Park, the site of the 2008 Summer Games. Every day tourists and other visitors stream through the park to look at the famous Bird's Nest and Water Cube. Some take pictures in front of these two buildings, while others simply wander around, appearing content to recreate the momentous events of that summer. Tourists who are asked why they flock to those buildings rarely talk about the buildings themselves. "That is where Mark Phelps won his Olympic record eight gold medals," they say, or, "That is where Usain Bolt ruled in the 100-meter dash."

People remember winners. In sports bars around the world, people quiz their friends about Super Bowl titlists, World Series champions, and World Cup winners. They remember Spain's run in the World Cup. They can recite the years the San Francisco 49ers won the Super Bowl, or how many championships the New York Yankees have won in their illustrious history. Ask them who finished second, and more often than not, you get silence in return. The occasional success still gets its due recognition, but the key places in our memory are held by those who build a record of sustained success over time. We remember the dynasties. It should make perfect sense, then, that this happens in the business world too. Successful companies fill the major plank of attention and analysis. Google, Microsoft, Apple, Facebook, and other leading firms receive the highest marks in credit and brand recognition.

Each generation has its own list of legendary icons, but a definitive answer to what sustains high levels of performance remains elusive. Perhaps we focus too much on the downstream, gazing at already-successful firms. We certainly tend to pay less attention to the upstream, seeking the early-stage differentiation that eventually separates the winners from the losers. Which of those firms will take their place in the next dynasty of market leadership? Have they already sowed the seeds of that future success?

These questions led us to the rough diamonds—the emerging market's most promising but still developing firms.

The kernel of this search began a few years ago when a group of respected entrepreneurs founded a new business school, Moscow School of Management SKOLKOVO, to develop future business leaders in Russia and other emerging markets. The idea of rough diamonds surfaced when Seung Ho Park started building a new think tank in collaboration with the school: the SKOLKOVO Institute for Emerging Market Studies. Since the ushering in of free market reform in emerging markets in the early 1980s, a cadre of firms—Gazprom and Rosneft (Russia), Infosys Tech and Tata Consultancy (India), Petrobras and Embraer S.A. (Brazil), and Sinopec and China Telecom (China)—had received a great deal of attention from the academic and business press. And rightly so: they're great companies. But Park and Wilfried Vanhonacker, the founding dean of the SKOLKOVO Business School, wondered what businesses would be in the next generation of successful firms. Can emerging markets produce the next business dynasties?

Over the next three years, Park and the IEMS research staff initiated the rough diamonds project with help from the Ernst & Young field offices in the BRIC countries (Brazil, Russia, India, and China). The methodology they employed was stringent and meticulous, so it took some time before a common set of enduring patterns emerged that accounted for sustained, profitable growth in all four countries. It is this story that unfolds in detail in this book.

We could not have finished this project without the inspiration of the exemplary business leaders in these emerging markets. In particular, we owe deep gratitude to Ruben Vardanian, a highly respected entrepreneur in Russia and a visionary leader of the SKOLKOVO Business School project. The global leadership and unbounded support of Ernst & Young helped see this project through to the end. The final phase of the project could not have been accomplished without the invaluable assistance of the editorial team at Jossey-Bass: Katherine D. Davies, Dan Zehr, Kathe Sweeney, Alina Poniewaz-Bolton, and Susan Geraghty. They were pivotal in facilitating the process and rewriting much of the original manuscript, which was laden with academic terms, into a readable and accessible final book.

Finally, we could not have accomplished a task of such magnitude without the enduring counsel and constant inspiration from our families. Ja Young, Alexandra, and Amelia Park patiently went through their activities while Seung Ho Park took off on frequent trips to emerging countries while working on this project. Nan Zhou thanks her family members, especially Yawei Wang, Shuiqing Zhou, and Jiajing Zhang for helping her concentrate on her research. Gerardo thanks his family for their constant support: Suki Ungson, Melissa and Tegan Martin, Carlo Riego, Mark Neveu, and Kaipo. Although it is impossible to completely express our appreciation for all they did to support us, as a small token of our gratitude we dedicate this book to them.

March 2013   Seung Ho Park
                                                  Moscow, Russia

                                                  Nan Zhou
                                                  Beijing, China

                                                  Gerardo R. Ungson
                                                  San Francisco, California

Acknowledgments

The project could not have been accomplished without the cooperation of all the firms that participated in the study and the assistance of countless people, including students, office staff, and Ernst & Young managers, who undertook various phases of the project. While a few sentences will not cover the entirety of all individuals to whom we owe a deep sense of appreciation, we particularly thank and acknowledge the following people who devoted time to help us in all four countries we studied: Kefei Zou, Jian Luo, Kino Li, Weidong Jin, Lin Yan, Jianbo Xu, Ruidong Shen, Yunliang Qiu, Alex Zhang, Nigel Knight, Utpal Almoula, Siva Prasad, Andre Ferreira, Sam Fouad, Hetal Pandya, Sandeep Gupta, Mansi Joshi, P. M. Murty, Siva Prasad, Padma Chourey, Namrata Datt, Farokh Balsara, M. S. Unnikrishnan, Vivek Gambhir, Abhishek Agrawal, Bhaskar Bhat, Harsh Mariwala, Ilgiz Baimuratov, Denis V. Shamening, Vladimir G. Borisov, Vitaly Korolev, Maria Agapkina, Aleksey Rybnikov, Alexander Filatov, Vladimir Nikolaevich Sungorkin, Prokhorov Konstantin Anatolevich, Irina Olegovna Samokhina, Alexander Storchak, Mikhail Bondarenko, Artur Davidyan, Alex Settles,

Liudmila Petrova, Thiago Borges, Raisa Vasilevna Demina, Viktor Gaiday, and Dmitry Voskoboynikov.

An earlier, abbreviated version of the book was distributed as a coauthored report, *Rough Diamonds: The 4Cs for Sustained High Performance*, by S. H. Park, N. Zhou, and G. Ungson for Ernst & Young. Portions of the project were also presented at the Davos Forum and the St. Petersburg Economic Summit in 2012.

Introduction

High performers take charge of their own destiny. They have a laser-sharp focus on executing against the four drivers of competitive success: customer reach, operational agility, cost competitiveness and stakeholder confidence. And they strike the right balance in their approach to each of these four drivers in relation to the others—strategically and tactically.

> —Ernst & Young, *Growing Beyond: How High Performers Are Competing for Growth in Difficult Times*

Much like legendary sports teams, development is not graded on current progress, but on the ability of these teams to produce a consistent flow of exemplary players over time. In context, newly competitive firms not only signal the future growth of emerging markets but also define the dynamism, vibrancy, and resilience of these economies over time.

> —SKOLKOVO Business School–Ernst & Young Institute for Emerging Market Studies, *Rough Diamonds: The 4Cs Framework for Sustained High Performance*

The global reach of the recent economic downturn prompted new questions about the sources of future business growth. Leaders of industry have long considered emerging markets a wellspring of new expansion opportunities, but slowing economies in even these countries have raised questions about their capacity for future prosperity and the challenges these markets pose for enterprising companies. Yet amid these challenges, a growing crop of powerful new private businesses—successful but largely unknown to those in developed markets—has started to mine considerable new opportunities. These are the rough diamonds, the exemplary breakout firms that are capitalizing on the developing nature of their home economies in Brazil, Russia, India, and China (the so-called BRIC countries, prized for their ongoing and potential economic growth).

These companies have clearly defined a new standard of excellence. They have established marked differentiation from established industry stalwarts and market leaders. They have set themselves up to sustain their growth well into the future. And they have lessons to impart to firms in other countries, both developed and developing markets. We wrote this book to profile and explain the remarkable performance and potential of these rough diamonds.

So what defines a rough diamond? For this book, we focused on the next generation of high-performing firms in the BRIC countries: the stars of the future. By many measures, these rough diamonds are the best-performing firms in the BRIC countries, operating at a level that exceeds many of the previously identified compilations of fast-growing companies. Taken as a whole, the rough diamonds companies have grown at an average rate of 43.12 percent over ten years, essentially doubling their sales every two years. In fact, China's rough diamonds doubled their growth every year and a half, an astonishing growth rate. Of course, growth alone cannot capture the full significance of a company's performance. In terms of profit margins and return on assets over an extended period of time, these rough diamonds match and often exceed the top five hundred private firms in their respective countries, not to mention the top twenty-five manufacturing firms in their countries and comparable firms worldwide.

Unlike the larger, renowned firms in each of these countries—Gazprom and Rosneft (Russia), Infosys Tech and Tata Consultancy (India), Petrobras and Embraer S.A. (Brazil), and Sinopec and China Telecom (China)—the rough diamonds have yet to attract much global attention. They are underrepresented in academic journals and the business press despite their exemplary performance. We wrote this book to put a spotlight on these hidden gems.

In chapter 1, we introduce the concept of rough diamonds and discuss the attributes that define these companies and their considerable potential for growth. Just as a real diamond's quality is defined by the four Cs—cut, color, clarity, and carat—the rough diamonds embody Four Cs that allow them to sustain their high performance: capitalize, create, craft, and cultivate. We discuss these attributes in chapter 2. In the succeeding four chapters, we detail each of the Four Cs using case studies to explain how rough diamonds differ from incumbent market leaders in the BRIC countries and in developed economies. Chapter 3 focuses on how rough diamonds capitalize on opportunities, notably government policies and industry transitions, in a period we call late development. Chapter 4 elaborates on how these firms create new markets by correctly identifying nascent consumer needs and consolidating them into viable market niches and segments. Chapter 5 offers a description of how rough diamonds craft operational excellence, most notably through integrated logistics, supply chain management, and supportive, resilient, and agile management systems. And in chapter 6, we focus on how rough diamonds cultivate profitable growth through strategies such as product diversification.

Combined, the Four Cs establish a platform for sustained profitable growth, and we develop that concept further in chapter 7, noting also the risks of the growth fetish or a misplaced goal of companies to grow for the sake of growth but without due consideration of consequences that many entrepreneurial enterprises fall prey to. And in chapter 8, we discuss the factors that drive hypergrowth in emerging markets, with a close look at the primary and secondary drivers that can sustain profitable growth over time.

Although rough diamonds share many of these defining characteristics, it would be misleading to suggest that companies don't conform to the unique intricacies of their home markets. Chapter 9 examines the country-specific differences the rough diamonds face, with an emphasis on the influence of historical, cultural, and institutional factors.

So why should anyone outside these BRIC markets pay attention to the rough diamonds? Simply put, they offer universal lessons for both academics and business leaders about how companies can succeed in these emerging markets and how they can spot and avoid the traps that threaten sustained growth. To compete in emerging markets requires a deep appreciation of local conditions that influence pent-up consumer demand and future consumption patterns. Entering emerging markets also requires a reassessment of conventional strategies and beliefs, which might work well in developed markets but often do not apply in evolving, underdeveloped economies. The success and future growth trajectories of rough diamonds increasingly foreshadow these new rules of the game for firms around the world. Understanding the performance of these exemplary firms provides important clues to the rich opportunities in the late-development era of the emerging BRIC markets.

We draw these lessons out in chapter 10, which offers our outlook on how rough diamonds have changed the game and provide recommendations for how companies around the world can tap the strategies of rough diamonds to forge success in the BRIC markets and beyond. This focus on breakout firms complements the prevailing direction in the literature on emerging markets, which seeks to identify the next developing economy that will drive future growth in the global economy. Undoubtedly defining the next growth market is a worthwhile effort. But our point of emphasis extends beyond that. We believe the sustained performance of any emerging market, now and in the future, will ultimately be determined by the dynamics that generate a constant flow of exemplary firms over time.

When we started adapting our research and reports to a book, we had both academics and business practitioners in mind. For academics, this study offers a complementary framework to reexamine conventional theories of business strategy and management systems. For researchers looking to gain a more nuanced understanding of emerging markets, the appendix provides details about our study methodology.

For business practitioners, knowing the extent to which these exemplary firms can sustain themselves provides critical insight into the sustainability of emerging economies over time. Specifically, the lessons gleaned from the rough diamonds help illuminate the very attributes of these emerging markets that facilitate and support these exemplary firms. A company that disregards or fights against these market factors will find itself vulnerable to competition, especially from the same firms they should be learning from. The multinational companies that understand and embrace the rough diamonds' motivations and aspirations will find complementary partners and key suppliers.

Finally, for readers of all stripes, learning more about rough diamonds helps illuminate important changes happening more broadly throughout the BRICs countries. Insight into how these companies forge their successes leads to an understanding of how the emerging markets' developing institutions, transitioning industrial development, new government policies, and shifting competitive frictions are taking these rough diamonds and polishing them into the brilliant gems they're poised to become.

1

An Overview

Better a diamond with a flaw than a pebble without one.

—Chinese proverb

Part of our western outlook stems from the scientific attitude and its method of isolating the parts of a phenomenon in order to analyze them.

—Arthur Ericson

The method of the enterprising is to plan with audacity and execute with vigor.

—Christian Nestell Bovee

How do real-world diamonds get their value? Part of it derives from their scarcity, but a host of other factors ultimately determines the extent to which a particular gem is prized. Rough diamonds are painstakingly cabbed, cut, and polished to remove infirmities, an intricate and rigorous process that leaves the diamond even more valuable than before. In this study, we employed a similarly rigorous method that involved numerous screening tests, comparison groups, and field interviews to help reveal the true value of the dynamic companies we examine in this book. This chapter details how we compiled our list of rough diamonds, and how they generate their value from internal (strategic) and external (market) factors.

Before Mindray Medical International sprang to life in 1991, the competitive landscape for the medical equipment industry in China resembled most other nascent technology markets in the country. Collections of foreign multinational brands dominated these sectors, trading off their considerable international reputation for quality and value. Yet despite the challenges, Mindray's leadership saw opportunities to take advantage of its local proximity, differentiate its products through a focus on innovation, and trade on its unwavering commitment to quality.

Based on its relationships with physicians and officials at local hospitals, the company targeted its research and development efforts and started focusing on being the first Chinese company to market home-grown, high-quality products. It started producing a string of Chinese firsts: the first Chinese-made blood-oxygen monitor, the first multiparameter monitor, and the first automatic blood cell analyzer. Mindray then turned around and emphasized the uniqueness of what it offered. It tapped into domestic pride by touting its locally manufactured products, and it offered its products at prices lower than those charged by the foreign brands. The differentiation advantage that had once been a strength for multinational firms largely vanished.

Mindray never lost its focus on innovation and quality. "Mindray holds the belief that very early innovation is our growth path," said Hang Xu, the company's president. "Quality is the door to our life." This commitment, which helped Mindray establish itself as a young company, now is helping the company continue its considerable growth. As of 2012, the company owned nine R&D centers around the world, including facilities in China, Seattle, New Jersey, and Stockholm. The same company that built on its home-grown reputation now has a global presence, and it has become one of the dominant brands in the Chinese medical equipment market by reversing the local bias from foreign products to domestic ones.

Mindray's story, largely unknown around the world, typifies a new, up-and-coming generation of private companies that's transforming markets in Brazil, Russia, India, and China—the BRIC nations. While these prized, high-growth markets have drawn keen interest from multinational companies, business journalists, and academics from virtually every corner of the global economy, this new crop of exemplary companies has emerged largely outside the glare of that spotlight. Yet they're posting incredible growth rates and offer an illuminating look at how companies, both foreign and domestic, can find new opportunities in these dynamic markets.

We call these companies *rough diamonds*. Although their prior growth has instilled an inherent value in their business, much like a diamond has an inherent value before it reaches the skilled hands of a gemologist, these companies are not flawless. They constantly burnish themselves against the difficulties and opportunities within the markets they serve. As Hang Xu of Mindray notes, "The medical equipment industry is different from those industries with a natural entry barrier—market and regulatory—of which none exists in the medical equipment industry . . . Therefore, we need to compete [with well-established competitors] to win the battles."

Yet much like Mindray Medical International, these rough diamonds have already taken on an unmistakable shine.

IDENTIFYING THE ROUGH DIAMONDS

We started our search for rough diamonds with a simple premise: identify the highest-performing private companies in the BRIC countries close to over a ten-year period from 2000 to 2009. (We focused on private companies because other types of firms, such as state-owned enterprises, might pursue other goals, such as administrative tasks.) Although the goal was straight-forward enough, reaching it required a much more arduous process. All told, we put hundreds of companies through a rigorous screening, employing multiple tests with increasingly strict standards, ultimately culling down the field to the finest collection of corporate gems.

This identification process relied primarily on a five-step process (which we describe in greater detail in the appendix). The first of these steps was intentionally broad, using multiple high-level measures of business performance, such as revenue growth, market share, profitability, and efficiency. Second, we put the hundreds of high-performance private companies that made the first cut through a more detailed, multitiered set of screens, including comparisons with comparable firms in the 2009 Top 500 in their countries and an in-depth frontier analysis, which is a way to evaluate a company's resource allocation efficiency.

Companies that met those standards advanced to the third step, in which we employed secondary data sources to help generate a template for what our rough diamonds should look like. And finally, for the fourth test, we hit the road to conduct extensive field interviews with leaders of many of the selected firms, building our understanding of their strategy, history, and potential.

With that, we had our preliminary list of rough diamonds, but we wanted to make sure we didn't lose an especially remarkable rough diamond because the technicalities of our process hid them from view. So we consulted with Ernst & Young on the validity of the data we used and solicited their expert feedback on the companies' management and strategic prowess. Based on this assessment, we added five firms, one in Russia and four in India, that field experts regarded as the best companies in their sectors.

And there you have it: after closely inspecting hundreds of companies and personally visiting dozens of them, we finally mined the seventy most promising rough diamonds: sixteen Chinese firms, sixteen Russian firms, twenty-two Indian firms, and sixteen Brazilian firms (table 1.1).

THE HIGH PERFORMANCE OF ROUGH DIAMONDS

Taken collectively, these seventy rough diamonds outperform not only competing firms within their respective BRIC countries but comparable firms in the global Top 500 list. In fact, as a group, these rough diamonds posted significantly higher sales growth and return-on-assets ratios than a broad range of other companies, including the top twenty-five manufacturing firms in their home countries, in the United States, and around the world (table 1.2).

Compared with the market leaders in their countries, the rough diamonds' growth rates are impressive. Consider the rough diamonds in China. Their ten-year average growth rate of 61.83 percent suggests that sales doubled every eighteen months. The average time it took rough diamonds in Russia (1.69 years), India (2.33), and Brazil (2.97) to double their sales was no less extraordinary. Equally important, this growth has not come at the expense of profitability; in all cases, the average return on assets was greater than the comparable

TABLE 1.1 The Rough Diamonds in the Study

Name	Industry	Average Efficiency*	Average Growth†	Average Profit‡	Market Rank§
China					
Anhui Yingliu Group	Precision steel casting	0.38	62.76%	10.41%	2
Beingmate	Baby products	0.43	77.23	7.75	5
Dongying Transis Textile	Textile	0.35	40.19	10.10	6
Hanking Group	Iron smelting	0.41	54.80	7.10	6
Hebei Risun Coking Group	Coking	0.41	64.24	8.28	7
Jinluo Group	Meat products	0.61	68.94	12.69	6
Jinglong Group	Solar photovoltaic	0.61	90.42	17.90	4
KTK Group	Locomotive parts	0.38	62.57	11.13	3
Linyang Group	Smart electric energy meters	0.47	68.05	9.14	1
Mindray Medical International	High-tech medical equipment	0.84	42.74	29.51	1
Qinghua Refractories	Refractory materials	0.51	75.12	9.34	1
Shandong Kingenta	Chemical fertilizer	0.36	58.95	7.43	3
Molong Petroleum Machinery	Oil and gas field machinery	0.37	56.62	11.35	1
Shengli Oilfield Highland	Petroleum exploring equipment	0.76	49.79	7.95	1
Wellhope Agri-Tech	Animal feed processing	0.57	41.17	10.90	1
Xiwang Group	Starch and starch products	0.41	68.18	6.88	2
Russia					
OZNA	Oil and gas equipment	0.37	37.32%	12.86%	6
Komsomolskaya Pravda	Publishing, printing, and equipment	0.37	35.00	9.88	1

MLVZ	Distilled and blended liquors	0.49	51.44	18.81	3
Sitronics Telecom	Telephone and telegraph apparatus	0.56	67.00	11.14	2
Sady Pridonya	Canned fruits and vegetables	0.70	75.00	25.45	3
TAVR	Sausages and other prepared meat	0.47	53.52	8.13	1
Topkinskii Tsement	Cement, hydraulic	0.72	44.89	23.58	4
Mordovtsement	Cement, hydraulic	0.46	36.68	19.45	2
MIUZ	Jewelry, precious metals	0.54	38.41	22.45	4
Velkom	Sausages and other prepared meats	0.68	75.00	12.50	3
NEP LL	Roasted coffee	0.42	36.00	11.47	1
Niiefa–Energo	Relays and industrial controls	0.49	37.03	14.90	3
Furniture Factory Maria	Furniture manufacturing	0.41	69.73	8.37	2
United Metallurgical Co.	Steel pipes and tubes	0.45	36.86	22.43	2
Slavyanka Plyus	Candy and other confectionery	0.57	62.00	13.53	2
Vimm–Bill–Dann Napitki	Canned fruits and vegetables	0.46	54.00	8.37	1
India					
Amara Raja Batteries	Storage batteries	0.45	27.10%	15.47%	2
Amtek India	Automotive components	0.50	42.60	29.40	6
Bombay Rayon Fashions	Cloth	0.54	70.04	13.20	3
Chettinad Cement	Cement	0.45	19.00	25.00	8
Godawari Power & Ispat	Power-driven hand tools	0.47	66.73	15.79	1
Lakshmi Machine Works	Textile machinery	0.49	17.85	15.61	1
Parekh Aluminex	Aluminum and aluminum products	0.65	37.77	13.39	4

(continued)

TABLE 1.1 (Continued)

Name	Industry	Average Efficiency*	Average Growth†	Average Profit‡	Market Rank§
Parle Biscuits	Bakery products	0.74	19.29	14.91	1
Ratnamani Metals & Tubes	Steel pipes and tubes	0.41	34.59	13.77	2
Sudhir Gensets	Motors and generators	0.50	29.00	14.00	5
Tata Metaliks	Pig iron	0.64	31.56	15.18	2
Thermax	Boilers and turbines	0.76	22.94	12.11	1
Vijai Electricals	Power, distribution, and transformers	0.54	38.57	14.98	1
Biocon	Pharmaceutical preparations	0.57	28.21	28.50	8
Sun Pharmaceutical	Pharmaceutical preparations	0.68	25.33	36.61	5
Godrej Consumer Products	Household and personal care products	0.99	33.32	19.54	8
Asian Paints	Paints, varnishes, and allied products	0.45	23.14	14.66	1
Sintex industries	Plastic products	0.50	46.93	18.34	6
Tata steel	Steel pipe and tubes	0.47	80.29	25.39	1
Hindalco industries	Primary production of aluminum	0.44	52.68	23.51	1
Titan	Watches and clocks	0.33	30.56	10.19	3
Marico	Household and consumer products	0.45	20.67	12.08	7
Brazil					
Açotubo	Steel pipe and tubes	0.68	32.23%	8.82%	2
Arezzo	Women's footwear, except athletic	0.66	41.23	10.10	2
Berneck	Special industry machinery	0.50	21.72	20.84	3

Company	Product	Efficiency score*	Growth in sales†	Growth in profit margin‡	Rank§
CBC Cartucho	Small arms ammunition	0.83	21.42	7.75	1
Cinpal	Iron and steel forgings	0.56	23.48	21.90	2
Ciser	Bolts, nuts, screws, rivets, and washers	0.58	24.05	14.21	2
Itambé	Cement, hydraulic	0.70	24.19	47.80	7
Coniexpress	Canned fruits and vegetables,	0.56	21.77	6.09	1
Esmaltec	Household cooking equipment	0.62	40.52	9.46	1
Forjas	Small arms	1.00	23.86	11.77	1
Renner	Women's, misses', and juniors' outerwear	1.00	25.81	9.21	1
Magnesita	Nonclay refractories	0.98	22.52	9.57	1
Natura	Perfumes, cosmetics, and toiletries	0.81	30.31	19.54	1
Randon	Truck trailers	0.89	25.70	12.80	1
Schulz	Air and gas compressors	0.99	24.06	6.05	1
WEG	Motors and generators	0.84	25.82	18.99	1

*The efficiency score is computed as the distance from the optimal allocation of resources using frontier analysis: the higher the score, the higher the efficiency.

†Growth in sales over the study period.

‡Growth in profit margin over the study period.

§Rank is determined by market share.

¶Due to data availability, the profit rate covers the period 2004 to 2009

TABLE 1.2   Comparison of Rough Diamonds and the Top
Twenty-Five Manufacturing Firms

	Average Sales Growth	Average Return on Assets*
Chinese rough diamonds	61.83%	16.01%
Chinese top twenty-five	41.10	7.27
Russia rough diamonds	50.62	21.36
Russia top twenty-five	20.62	8.83
India rough diamonds	34.72	19.80
India top twenty-five	31.02	8.82
Brazil rough diamonds	26.36	15.41
Brazil top twenty-five	37.75	4.34
U.S. top twenty-five	8.50	8.84
Worldwide top twenty-five	9.45	4.92
Fortune 500	12.90	3.70

Note: The time period for China and Russia is ten years; for Brazil, seven years; and for India, nine years.
*Given that the comparative group comprises manufacturing firms, return on assets was used as the appropriate measure.

groups of companies. In fact, the rough diamonds in three countries collectively outperformed the comparable top twenty-five manufacturing firms in terms of both sales growth and profitability. (Brazil was the lone exception: Brazilian rough diamonds tend to be older firms, so their maturity tends to limit their opportunities for sales growth. However, the core competencies these same companies built over their longer histories have produced considerably higher profits.)

No matter how we sliced the comparisons, even when up against the archetype of business achievement, the Fortune 500 list, these companies collectively posted greater numbers for growth, profitability, and a range of other measures (table 1.3). Simply put, the rough diamonds have already transformed the

TABLE 1.3 Comparison of Rough Diamonds and Top 500 Firms (ten-year averages)

Variable	Top 500 Firms (Mean)	Rough Diamonds (Mean)
China		
Capital (natural logarithm of million US dollars)	11.82	11.41
Employees (natural logarithm of the number of employees)	7.60	7.47
Age (years)	15.63	15.31
Efficiency	0.33	0.47
Sales growth	39.44%	61.83%
Return on assets	11.25%	16.01%
Profit margin	6.71%	10.96%
Market share	1.61%	1.96%
Russia		
Capital	9.52	9.22
Age	29.31	18.36
Efficiency	0.33	0.51
Sales growth	29.63%	50.62%
Return on assets	10.83%	21.36%
Profit margin	6.59%	15.21%
Market share	5.98%	4.29%
India		
Capital	3.20	3.56
Age	33.48	25.59
Efficiency	0.40	0.55
Sales growth	16.99%	34.72%
Return on assets	9.04%	19.80%
Profit margin	11.27%	18.26%
Market share	9.56%	15.90%[a]
Brazil		
Capital	4.31	4.78
Age	31.67	49.60
Efficiency	0.50	0.77

(continued)

TABLE 1.3   *(Continued)*

Variable	Top 500 Firms (Mean)	Rough Diamonds (Mean)
Sales growth	21.15%	26.36%
Return on assets	7.79%	15.41%
Profit margin	5.34%	14.68%
Market share	3.18%	6.55%

Note: The market shares of Chinese and Russian firms are calculated based on almost the whole population of firms in each industry. The market shares of Indian and Brazil firms are calculated by CMIE and ORBIS data sets that do not fully reflect the industry structure.

competitive landscape in the BRIC markets. Those changes will become all the more remarkable in the coming years.

THE EVOLVING LANDSCAPE IN THE BRIC COUNTRIES

To get a better sense for how dramatic a transformation these rough diamonds are generating, it helps to first understand the remarkable changes already occurring in developing countries. For decades, the industrial landscape in most emerging economies was dominated by state-owned enterprises and heavily regulated companies. Only in the past two decades has the confluence of three key factors—market liberalization, technological advances, and globalization—accelerated the integration of more emerging economies into the global economy.

In the early 1980s, state-owned enterprises and regulated exporters drove almost all the global initiatives coming from most of these developing markets. To be sure, these state-owned companies will remain a fixture in many emerging markets for the foreseeable future. But as these countries started liberalizing their markets and privatizing seminal industries, the influence of profit-driven, efficiency-focused, and market-oriented private companies started driving a new era of economic development. Bereft of significant assistance and resources from a central government, these private firms had to be more entrepreneurial and less conventional, often resembling attributes of the break-out start-ups in developed economies.

In that context, this new wave of rough diamonds offers a unique view not only of the ongoing evolution of emerging markets around the world, but how these firms and markets compare and contrast with developed economies and top global companies (box 1.1).

Like any other broad assessment, this one comes with a caveat: assessing the performance of private firms in emerging markets is a daunting task. First, reliable data are hard to come by. Stock markets in emerging markets are newly developed and not well regulated. As a result, questions arise about the accuracy and, given recent scandals about stock price manipulation and insider trading in some markets, the legitimacy of financial market data.[1] The second challenge is the limited number of publicly listed companies. Chinese stock exchanges, for example, list only about two thousand of the millions of firms operating in the country. To account for these limitations, we used more conservative accounting measures than the financial market data typically used in studies of developed economies.

ROUGH DIAMONDS PROPEL EMERGING MARKETS

Despite the challenges that emerging markets can present to businesses inside and outside those countries, the population and economic growth rates in these countries make

Box 1.1 How Entrepreneurship Is Different in Emerging Markets

The word *entrepreneur* has been around since at least the early 1700s, but the theoretical underpinning for how we regard the term today stemmed from the work of twentieth-century Austrian economist Joseph Schumpeter. Schumpeter argued that the entrepreneur is the agent of change and dynamism in market capitalism. Because entrepreneurs engage in new ventures, he said, they invariably disrupt the existing order. Without what Schumpeter famously called "creative destruction," growth would be limited, and capitalism would stagnate.

The attributes of today's entrepreneurs have become a common vernacular across political boundaries: visionaries, risk takers, tireless, passionate, irreverent, tenacious, game changers, and so on. The terms conjure up images of luminaries in a broad range of industries. Steve Jobs, Fred Smith, Sergy Brin, Phil Knight, Sam Walton, Ingvar Kamprad, Soichiro Honda, Percy Barnevik, and Pierre Omidyar: all of them embody these characteristics.

So how do entrepreneurs from emerging markets differ from their well-publicized counterparts in developed countries? They do, of course, share many of the same attributes. However, the context within which they exert their creative energies necessarily influences their entrepreneurial strategies and tactics. We found that the leaders of the rough diamonds excelled at several things that entrepreneurs in developed markets rarely face (or deal with in vastly different circumstances):

- *Nurturing close relationships with government*. Rough diamonds are private firms, but this did not dissuade them from working closely with the public sector.
- *Establishing relational capital*. Rough diamonds work extensively with their contacts and networks, partly for accessing capital and partly for assistance in their business ventures.
- *Turning disadvantages into advantages*. Not unlike their counterparts in developed countries, rough diamonds are game breakers. But in emerging markets, entrepreneurs often manifest that by entering niches in established or maturing markets.
- *Being creative late, but also as early entrants*. What appears contradictory actually makes sense to rough diamonds; indeed, they are late in

terms of entering markets with established incumbents, but they're early in that they aggressively tackle markets with still undefined or evolving demand.

- *Avoidance of publicity*. Rough diamonds generally eschew uninvited visibility and attention.

them too promising for companies to resist. The prominence and promise of Brazil, Russia, India, and China have already spurred a new quest to identify the next set of surging markets and breakout nations. BRIC has been joined by a whole parade of acronyms; just the sound of "Next-11," "CIVETS," and "VISTA" hints at some untold potential for growth.[2] The telltale book titles already embedded in the business lexicon—*Breakout Nations, Growth Map*—invite the same interest and heighten expectations even further.[3]

Given the sluggish world economy in 2012, however, a new line of the story started to pop up. While pundits see new growth in emerging markets as the key to a global recovery, questions about the sustainability of their economic expansion, currently projected to outpace developed economies by 3.5 percent, remain unanswered.[4] Can those soaring rates be sustained into the future? Will companies still be able to find new opportunities going forward?

These emerging economies will continue to grow and offer rich business opportunities. But their ongoing development will rely in large part on rough diamonds and companies like them. All told, we examined more than 105,000 companies throughout the BRIC countries. The revenues and profits of the seventy rough diamonds we identified grew faster, and in a more sustainable manner, than the rest. Even beyond the specific lessons we can learn from their experiences, it's clear that these companies are opening up economic opportunities across entire emerging markets.

GROW, AND GROW ALIKE

These exemplary firms don't exist to help their national economies expand. They've done plenty to capitalize on the booming home markets too. Few have done that as successfully as Yonghua Lu, who founded the Linyang Group in 1997. At the time, Lu was a successful manager of a computer firm, earning an annual salary of more than 1 million RMB (about $160,000). But when he learned that a joint venture he had recommended, a little proposal called Linyang Electronics, had lost about 1 million RMB and was teetering on the edge of bankruptcy, he decided to give up his comfortable job and revive the project. He quit and bought out the equity shares of the joint venture.

It was a risky decision. The fledgling firm had no technology, no capital, and no customers. Undaunted, Lu bought a second-hand van and traveled extensively throughout China, exploring patterns in consumer demands and weaving them into his new vision for Linyang. By the end of the first year, he had the kernel for his first big product launch: Lu predicted that many aspiring households in China would want to upgrade their electric meters. He built a smart, single-phase electronic meter that clicked with the country's rising middle class. Linyang was a success.

By 2004, Lu was noticing a new pattern emerging with China's increasing affluence and growth and steered the company toward a new market—one with great potential but still largely untested: solar energy. The soaring growth of China's infrastructure that followed the move proved his new venture, Linyang Solarfun, was yet another timely response to the demands of a growing market. In just two years, Linyang Solarfun's revenue reached $60 million, and on December 21, 2006, it went public on the NASDAQ exchange, raising $150 million. Not content to sit on his laurels, Lu sold all of his shares in 2010 and has since entered another promising industry: power storage. For all that Lu gained from China's remarkable ascension over the past fifteen years, his ability to identify new opportunities proves that it takes much more than a soaring economy to find success in these emerging markets.

BEYOND EXEMPLARY FIRMS, WHAT IS REALLY DIFFERENT?

Studying the distinctive characteristics of exemplary firms might not strike some readers as especially novel. After all, a number of bestselling books have already done this exercise for firms in both developed and emerging markets. In most cases, the characteristics that set exemplary young companies apart tend to be quite similar from country to country. For example, the strong up-and-coming firms tend to focus on strategic planning, market development, and relentless implementation no matter which market they call home.

So what is really different about this study? Rather than look solely at the factors that drive the growth of exemplary businesses, we delved into a subject of deep interest to keen observers of emerging markets: how these rough diamonds sustain their growth over time. Any emerging market might be of particular interest at a certain time, but observers will question whether it can sustain growth and prosperity.

Pundits and politicians typically view sustained growth through a historical lens, emphasizing macroeconomic projections that are tied to past performance. Emerging markets are expected to maintain growth as long as the economic drivers that underpinned their past performance remain stable and continue to expand. However, this approach fails to fully capture the complexities of many institutional developments, such as improvements in education, legal systems, or infrastructure. They emphasize quantitative growth, not systemic development (box 1.2.).[5]

We adopted a different approach for this study, one that specifically focuses on sustainable growth from the standpoint of new and evolving players. Like great sports franchises, development is graded not on one game's performance but on the organization's ability to develop exemplary players who can win over the long haul. The sustained performance of the rough diamonds portends not only the future growth of emerging markets, but the future development of a dynamic, vibrant, and resilient economy over time. It is systemic in that it facilitates an analysis of exemplary firms over a long period of time. Moreover, because exemplary firms over time tend to be embedded in supportive institutions, we view development in both quantitative and qualitative terms, providing a platform for examining how development can be both systemic and synergistic in an emerging market economy.

The many rough diamonds profiled throughout this book offer remarkably varied stories of success that encompass individual endeavors as well as institutional development. They provide a different set of lenses for understanding sustained growth and high performance. Yet by looking at rough diamonds as a group, we can start to identify common patterns that

can benefit companies of all stripes. Collectively, their remarkable growth tends to emerge from a progressive sequence of
four primary strategies.

We call them the Four Cs.

Box 1.2 What Is "Development" in an Emerging Market Economy?

The potential of emerging markets has spawned numerous treatises about
what actually qualifies as one. Based on an extensive review of the literature,
the SKOLKOVO Business School–Ernst & Young Institute for Emerging Market
Studies distilled the following characteristics:

- *Rapid growth*. Distinctly faster growth rates distinguish emerging markets from the developed ones. While developed economies grow at an
  average of roughly 2.5 percent a year, emerging markets can grow as
  much as two or three times this rate, depending on which forecasting
  source is cited. Typically an annual growth rate of 5 percent is the
  standard for emerging markets.
- *Relatively lower economic development*. Compared with established
  economies, emerging markets are still in the process of development.
  Hence, market and capitalistic institutions are not as adequately developed, and governments are generally more interventionist during this
  transitional process.
- *Potential for continued high growth*. Not all emerging markets exhibit
  the rates of growth associated with fast-growing economies, but they
  have the observable potential to realize such levels in the foreseeable
  future. Hence, emerging markets also present propitious opportunities
  for growth as they evolve into more developed economies.

While critics will debate this point, we believe that emerging markets also
exhibit a greater likelihood to establish and nurture property and human rights
and become more capitalistic in orientation. Without these institutions, many
experts argue, development will be stunted and future growth limited. When

viewing growth in this context, development in emerging markets tends to be systemic and synergistic over time.

Sources: Adapted from William T. Wilson and Nicolay Ushakov, "Brave New World Categorizing the Emerging Market Economies — A New Methodology," SKOLKOVO Emerging Market Index (February 2011, June 2012). Sources cited in this report in support of the arguments include Eden Lorraine, "The Rise of Transnational Corporations from Emerging Markets: Threat or Opportunity?" in *Rise of Transnational Corporations from Emerging Markets*, ed. Karl P. Sauvant (Northampton, MA: Edward Elgar Publishing, 2008); Khanna Tarun, Krishna G. Palepu, and Richard J. Bullock, *Winning in Emerging Markets: A Road Map for Strategy and Execution* (Boston: Harvard Business Press, 2010); Sunje Aziz and Civi Emin, "Emerging Markets: A Review of Conceptual Frameworks," in *Proceedings of the First International Joint Symposium on Business Administrator: Challenges for Business Administrators in the New Millennium* (Canakkale Onsekiz Mart Universitz, Silesian University, Gokceade Canakkale, Turkey, 2008); and Dilip K. Das, *Financial Globalization and the Emerging Market Economies* (London: Routledge Taylor and Francis, 2004).

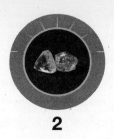

2

The Four Cs of High Performance

Breakout is a forceful emergence from a restrictive form or position. It is a structured and purposeful approach to corporate change and market or industry transformation, leading to dramatic performance improvements and business success.

> —Sidney Finkelstein, Charles Harvey, and Thomas Lawton,
> *Breakout Strategy: Meeting the Challenge of Double-Digit Growth*

Not unlike real-world rough diamonds [RDs], the transformation of RD firms . . . entails meticulous strategies and purposeful actions. After careful assessment of our case studies and interviews, we propose a trajectory that is best characterized by a sequential composite strategy—one we term the Four Cs for Sustaining High Performance.

> —SKOLKOVO Business School–Ernst & Young Institute
> for Emerging Markets, *Rough Diamonds: The 4Cs Framework for Sustained High Performance*

The details that lead to success vary widely from industry to industry, country to country, and company to company. That's especially true for high-growth firms in emerging markets. But meticulous consideration of the rough diamonds starts to reveal some telling commonalities about their paths to success. We distilled these into a progressive sequence of four interrelated strategies shared by all of these firms. We call them the Four Cs: *capitalizing* on late development,[1] *creating* inclusive market niches and segments, *crafting* operational excellence, and *cultivating* profitable growth.

A mined diamond shares little resemblance to the stunning gems that adorn rings, expensive necklaces, and other fine jewelry. Going from rough diamonds to sparkling finished stones involves a delicate multistep process that requires intense skill, keen knowledge, proper tools, and extensive experience. Gem cutters set out to craft a finished gem with specific angles and facets, all of which combine to bring out the luster and fire for which diamonds are so highly prized.

Yet the intricate skill of the cutter determines only part of the diamond's ultimate price. The four Cs that define a diamond's value—carat, cut, color, and clarity—stem from attributes embodied in the stone, as well as the cutter's own talent. It's the balance of these four qualities that ultimately establishes the quality of the diamond.

The same holds true for companies in emerging markets. Like the gem cutter who recognizes the qualities and flaws of the rough stone and cuts accordingly, the leaders of rough diamond companies use both their skill and the opportunities and the barriers of their marketplace to create a thriving business.

Business leaders in emerging markets have to pay special attention to the significant challenges inherent in an under-developed economy. Rough diamonds in emerging markets typically don't have the advantage of established institutional environments, yet they almost always find themselves pitted against large, established competitors—both foreign and domestic (box 2.1). Far from being dissuaded, these firms used the

Box 2.1 The Context of Development in Emerging Markets

Researchers, political officials, and business leaders often employ different criteria to distinguish emerging and developed markets. One of the more intriguing distinctions is that proposed by Harvard University professors Tarun Khanna and Krishna Palepu, who argue that emerging markets lack the critical specialized institutions that enable and facilitate market-based transactions. This condition gives rise to what they call "institutional voids."

Unlike in developed economies, where buyers and sellers can readily come together, such parties in emerging markets lack the intermediaries who facilitate the anticipated transactions. Buyers and sellers often are inhibited by a lack of information, inadequate distribution channels, untenable physical infrastructure, or an unacceptable dispute resolution process. And without supportive institutions, transaction costs tend to rise significantly higher than in developed economies. Ultimately the absence of market intermediaries can limit demand, mute market signals, hamper infrastructure, and skew market incentives.

Because of the lack of full-fledged market-based institutions, nonmarket structures have arisen in their stead. For example, as Khanna and Palepu note, large-scale conglomerates, such as the Japanese *keiretsu* and the Korean *chaebol*, now function as internal capital markets. In lieu of more established market-based capital sources, these conglomerates allocate capital to members (smaller firms) within their respective industrial groups.

In this way, capital advantages tend to accrue to domestic firms, which have a much deeper grasp of the local conditions than foreign firms do. Absent a deep understanding of such institutional voids, any prospective firm seeking to operate in emerging markets will quickly find itself at a severe disadvantage. Even so, with an appreciation of these voids and the know-how of redressing them, foreign and domestic firms can start to fill these voids with market-based institutions and create their own unique competitive advantages.

Sources: Adapted from Tarun Khanna and Krishna Palepu, *Winning in Emergent Markets: A Roadmap for Strategy and Execution* (Boston: Harvard Business School Publishing, 2010), and Tarun Khanna and Krishna Palepu, "Why Focused Strategies May Be Wrong for Emerging Markets," *Harvard Business Review* (July-August 1997): 41–51.

challenges they faced not only as motivation but also as a fundamental rationale for their activities. They took their cue from English author G. K. Chesterton, who wrote, "An adventure is only an inconvenience rightly considered. An inconvenience is an adventure wrongly considered." The seventy rough diamonds profiled in this book have distinguished themselves by successfully bridging the macroeconomic evolution ongoing in their markets with a set of firm-specific strategies at the micro-operational level.

THE FOUR Cs FOR SUSTAINING HIGH PERFORMANCE

Like the four Cs of diamond quality, we identified a set of four progressive and interrelated strategies that have produced such high levels of quality among our rough diamonds. Although different companies relied more or less on each of the individual Four Cs we've established, all of them shared an ability to blend these strategies in a way that produced rapid and, more important, sustained growth (figure 2.1). By multiple measures, these firms have been able to sustain their exceptionally high level of performance for a decade. This long-term sales growth and profitability separate the rough diamonds from the rest.

Capitalizing on Late Development
Rough diamonds can look at the established market and identify new growth segments, unattended niches, or unfilled institutional voids that provide a rationale for their entry. Such opportunities arise from favorable government regulations and policies (e.g., market liberalization, incentives for privatization, or import substitution) and from industry transitions (e.g., the

FIGURE 2.1   The Four Cs for Sustaining High Performance

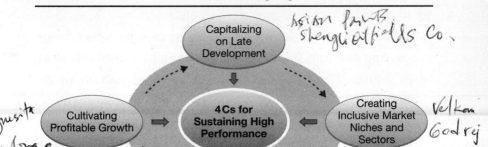

maturation of certain markets that impel leading companies to abandon or deemphasize some current segments).

This is far from a straightforward process. These niches aren't easily spotted, and the opportunities are not easily exploitable. Rough diamonds have to be discerning trend spotters—not in the sense of identifying radically new markets or product applications but in their willingness to invest in previously neglected niches. Moreover, they have to muster their expertise at accessing resources at the early stage of development, adopting a sort of internal entrepreneurship that capitalizes on their relationships, technological advantages, or organizational flexibility. By exercising their vision, focus, and willingness to take risks, these business leaders mirror the traits of exemplary entrepreneurs in developed markets.

Creating Inclusive Market Niches and Segments
The rough diamonds are especially adept at responding to changing consumer demands, nurturing their local connections, building advantages through differentiation, and

consolidating previously fragmented market niches. In doing so, they create inclusive growth markets.

Conventional marketing in advanced countries focuses on generating demand for an established or a new product. More often than not, entry is based on the size and viability of the market segment in question. Compared with their larger counterparts in advanced economies, rough diamonds have little control over these factors. Rather, they have to find ways to consolidate or aggregate overlooked pockets of demand in existing markets. Whether these niches are fragmented due to geographical, cultural, or financial factors, rough diamonds typically blanket these nascent markets with aggressive programs that build awareness of their products and services and foster deep consumer loyalty.

Crafting Operational Excellence

After securing market position, rough diamonds go through a critical process of building their core competencies in order to sustain performance and prepare for the next phase of market expansion. In any emerging market, there is no one-size-fits-all approach. In the BRIC countries, each rough diamond crafted a mix of its company's abilities and resources to drive strategies and consolidate market position.[2]

This process requires that rough diamonds tap into the advantages they have, or can build, at every stage of the value chain: sourcing network efficiencies, supply chain logistics management, operational efficiencies, stringent quality standards, collaborative innovation, and dynamic and resilient organizational structures and processes. Underlying all of these efforts is a purposeful learning strategy that includes everything from coordinated research with universities, to informal networks, to selective joint ventures.

Cultivating Profitable Growth

Finally, rough diamonds leverage these internal competencies through a phased, scaled market expansion. In many cases, this includes an incremental expansion into international markets, but always with a relentless focus on achieving world-class standards. Rough diamonds tend to take different approaches to their overall growth strategies depending on the opportunities and constraints they face. Some are more aggressive than others, but virtually all of them take a balanced approach that does not overtax their internal resources and doesn't incur unnecessary risks. In other words, they focus on sustained growth over time.

PUTTING THE FOUR Cs TO WORK

Forjas doesn't immediately pop out as a typical high-growth firm. The Brazilian company was founded in 1937 as a tool and die manufacturer, not necessarily the first impression when you think of emerging markets. Yet over the decades, Forjas transformed itself into a broader industrial conglomerate now known as one of the world's leading weapons and armaments companies. (In the United States, it's better known as Taurus USA.)

The firm initially acquired its knowledge from Smith & Wesson, a widely known brand and an established arms manufacturer. In fact, much of Forjas's initial capital came from Smith & Wesson, which had acquired Forjas shares. Eventually the Brazilian firm Polimeta reacquired the equity stake and, in effect, renationalized the company. With a renewed level of independence in the ensuing decades, Forjas systematically diversified its product offerings and established itself as a major supplier to the Brazilian government, which started replacing foreign arms imports with this reliable local supplier.

Since establishing itself, Forjas has forged even stronger bonds with the government. Beyond becoming a reliable supplier of armaments, it has delivered a continuous stream of innovative products, including technological skills and training programs, that aligned with evolving national interests and built an increasing level of international brand prestige.

Like virtually all our other seventy rough diamonds, Forjas took advantage of late development (capitalize), built new growth segments (create), constantly upgraded its internal skills and resources (craft), and consolidated its position establishing its expertise in core markets while pushing innovation in new markets (cultivate). As we will see in the next four chapters, each of these sequential Four C steps helps provide a common foundation for understanding how these rough diamonds create incredible value (table 2.1).

To be sure, each firm has a different focus and a different portfolio. While we emphasize their common attributes, rough diamonds of course adopt modifications or refinements of these strategies depending on their unique environmental and internal contingencies. Yet every one of them takes an intensive entrepreneurial approach to their business that's reflected in the Four Cs and equally instructive for companies in developed and emerging markets alike.

TABLE 2.1 Overview of the Four Cs

Characteristics	Capitalizing on Late Development	Creating Inclusive Market Niches and Segments	Crafting Operational Excellence	Cultivating Profitable Growth
Description	Exploiting opportunities arising from government policies and industry dynamics	Building exclusive growth markets by consolidating fragmented demand and filling in underserved market niches	Building operational excellence in all stages of the firm's value chain	Managing growth domestically and internationally
Underlying logic	Entrepreneurial	Market development	Operational excellence, core competence	Growth, leverage, and expansion
Key drivers	Capitalize on favorable government policies Exhibit relentless passion in adversity Excel at relational or technological expertise	Anticipate and respond to consumer expectations Consolidate fragmented niches and segments Develop deep differentiation advantages Take advantage of first-mover strategies	Excel in integrated logistics and supply chain management Nurture collaborative innovation Be stringent in total quality assurance Build flexible, agile, and cohesive management	Patterns of product diversification China: Mobilize relational capital Brazil: Attention to gradual diversification Russia: Focus on domestic growth India: Focus on sustained international growth

3

Capitalizing on Late Development

The visionaries in RDs [rough diamonds] have a sense of market niches that are underserved, consumer needs that are evolving, and industry changes that are transformative. While they might be latecomers as leaders in market competition, they exemplify a unique type of entrepreneurship that combines risk taking, creative learning, and bold execution.

Industrial evolution in emerging markets is much subtler in context, more nuanced in scale, and more incremental in growth. Development gives rise to early market leaders, but with accelerating competitive pressures, new opportunities are created for other more efficient firms.

—SKOLKOVO Business School–Ernst & Young Institute for Emerging Market Studies, *Rough Diamonds: The 4Cs Framework for Sustained High Performance,*

Compared with their peers, rough diamonds are better at recognizing market opportunities that arise from late development. They can do this because they display three critical attributes: they capitalize on favorable government policy, exhibit relentless passion in adversity, and excel at building their relationships or technological expertise, or both. These capabilities exemplify a rare type of entrepreneurship in emerging markets.

Observers typically think of development as a progression from primitive states toward modern economies. Their perspective sees the lack of development in emerging markets as a static situation that should generally be remedied by imitating the experiences of their more developed counterparts.[1] Everyone, in essence, follows the same general path toward development.

Rough diamonds see the world differently. The visionary leaders of these companies recognize the underserved market niches, the changing consumer needs, and the industry fluctuations that emerge in a market's later stages of development. They capitalize on these opportunities to create revolutionary, rather than evolutionary, transitions in the markets they serve.

So while rough diamonds might be latecomers to the battle for market leadership, they exemplify a unique type of entrepreneurship that capitalizes on overlooked opportunities by combining risk taking, creative learning, and bold execution. And make no mistake: their ability to ascertain changes is not fleeting. Rough diamonds are distinguished—in fact, often defined—by their visionary and entrepreneurial skills.

Simply put, rough diamonds don't follow the same old path to development. Instead, they capitalize on the changes that emerge during the late development of the markets they serve (see box 3.1).

Box 3.1 The Dynamics of Late Development

The First Industrial Revolution (1750–1850) transformed England from its agricultural and feudalistic roots to a thriving, commercial, and market-based society. But like any other major transformation in the world economy, this one had its own defining characteristics related to its changing institutions and technologies. In England, for example, the invention of the spinning jenny and steam power, the emergence of the factory system, the growing supply of workers arising partly from the enclosure movement, a more educated population, and the advent of market-based capitalism underpinned the broader economic changes occurring across society.

The Second Industrial Revolution that encompassed North America, Western Europe, and Japan in the late 1880s ushered in novel methods of mass production, an awareness of marketing and consumerism, and the modern market-based system. Economic historian Alice Amsden describes the late-1980s emergence of South Korea, Singapore, Hong Kong, and Taiwan as "late industrialization" and "late development," both of which were facilitated by education and learning trajectories. Other scholars, such as Antoine van Agtmael, would later extend Amsden's arguments to include the experiences and development of local market leaders in emerging markets.

We've adopted Amsden's term, *late development*, to describe the experience of rough diamonds. It underscores the key differences between the initial market leaders in emerging economies and the surge of potential successful upstarts. In this context, "lateness" does not refer to the age of a firm. Rather, it refers to the time when the company assumed a market leadership position. Unlike previous events that were demarcated by a few revolutionary developments, both technological and institutional, the process of late development is a confluence of many factors. Industrial evolution in emerging markets is much subtler in context, more nuanced in scale, and more incremental in growth. Development in these markets gives rise to early market leaders. But as competitive pressures accelerate, new opportunities open up for more efficient firms. The rough diamonds do not enter such niches arbitrarily but come prepared through investment in technology, relationships or operating efficiency.

Sources: Alice Amsden, *Asia's Next Giant: South Korea and Late Industrialization* (New York: Oxford University Press, 1989); Antoine van Agtmael, *The Emerging Markets Century* (New York: Free Press, 2007); and Anita McGahan, *How Industries Evolve: Principles for Achieving and Sustaining Superior Performance* (Boston: Harvard Business School Press, 2004).

SOURCES OF OPPORTUNITY IN LATE DEVELOPMENT

In these later stages, opportunities tend to grow out of two primary sources. The first stems from changes in government policy. In most emerging countries, new policies tend to arise out of moves to liberalize markets, stimulate privatization, or encourage the replacement of imports with local products. As the rules that govern a market change, astute observers see new doorways opening to previously unattended markets. Rough diamonds walk through those doors.

The second source emerges when industry development starts to change consumer demand. These typically arise as a market matures and leading companies start to abandon or deemphasize certain segments. However, rather than simply pick up the scraps left behind by larger competitors, rough diamonds use these openings as a portal for market entry and then build or consolidate segments with innovative products, services, or value. Especially when compared with other firms, rough diamonds better recognize these emerging sectors and nascent niches, where basic market features have yet to coalesce and build them into a viable and profitable business.

Rough diamonds not only recognized these government policy changes and industry developments; they jumped in with opportunistic ventures that have generated remarkable returns over the long haul.

ROUGH DIAMONDS CAPITALIZE ON FAVORABLE GOVERNMENT POLICY

Since China adopted its open door policy in 1978, a host of private firms have emerged. One widespread type of private firm is the town-village-owned enterprise (TVE). The government purposefully encouraged villagers to engage in manufacturing as a strategy to absorb the excess labor from the agrarian sector. It was among the first overtures to replace the planned economy in parts of China with a market system. In the late 1970s and early 1980s, these TVEs became the first private firms in China; some of the Chinese rough diamonds are among them. But because it was such a radical change some of the TVE leaders didn't see it as a panacea and failed to avail themselves of the full benefits of market inclusion.

One exception has become a prominent rough diamond firm. The Qinghua Group had the foresight to combine its locational advantages with favorable government policies. The Yingkou Qinghua Group started in 1984 as a modest production team in Qinghuayu, a village in Yingkou County, Liaoning Province. The village sits in an area with a large amount of magnesium reserves—all told, 2.56 billion tons, including 1.12 billion tons good for industry use. The Yingkou magnesium reserve in fact accounts for a quarter of the world's supply.

Sitting on such an abundant natural resource, the Qinghua Group embraced the new government policies and developed itself into the largest refractory material manufacturer in China. Over our study period, the company posted dazzling average annual revenue growth of almost 74 percent, and total revenue hit 9.4 billion RMB in 2010 ($1.5 billion).

TVEs weren't the only type of private company to emerge from China's market liberalization. In the 1980s and early 1990s, China adopted a policy of "grasping the large, releasing the small" to transform many of its smaller state-owned enterprises into private companies. Many of them have become prominent rough diamonds.

Two examples are noteworthy. The first is the Shengli Oilfield Highland Petroleum Equipment company, which exemplifies how strong leadership can capitalize on privatization. After losing money every year before Xianping Yang took charge in 1998, the company needed someone who better understood the new nature of business in a more liberal market. Yang, an expert in petroleum equipment with almost thirty years of experience, leaned on his business and managerial experience, along with a keen sense of the government's interest in the success of former state-owned enterprises that had been privatized, to reorganize and rebuild the company for the new environment. Within three years, he had reversed the firm's losses and started generating a profit. Over our study period, the company posted an average annual sales growth of nearly 50 percent.

The second example, Shandong Molong Petroleum Machinery, owes its legacy to its founder, Enrong Zhang, who was born in the countryside and received little formal education. When selected by a local party chief to assume oversight of the struggling town-owned agricultural machine repair plant, Zhang set to work on rebuilding the company. With the easing of policies to facilitate privatization, Zhang was able to purchase

60 percent of the firm's equity, taking an interest not only in the company but in its success as well.

He helped better connect Molong with the massive China National Petroleum Corp. (CNPC) and tap into its wide distribution to other markets. The company also benefited from the presence of Shandong's other booming industries, which provided key supplies and materials. But at its core, the Chinese government's shift toward privatization—and Zhang's subsequent ability to take an ownership stake in the firm—set the stage for the company's success. Said Yunliang Qiu, Ernst & Young's former supervisor with the Molong Project, "Molong benefited from the loosening of regulations over the company, implicit in the opening and reform policy. If not for privatization, the firm would not have materialized."

As privatization opened the door for many rough diamonds, government policies designed to encourage the replacement of imports with domestically produced products also created new market opportunities. Usually experts regard import substitution as antidevelopment. It is, they argue, a protectionist move designed to do little more than shield local markets. The preferred option, exporting, would ensure entry into global markets without closing the door to products that might not be available in the local markets otherwise.

Nevertheless, import substitution has come to be increasingly recognized as a strategy that can promote a degree of self-sufficiency and reduce a market's dependence on imported goods, especially important if the prices of these goods are high. Import substitution is not inherently flawed; it can be effective if applied in appropriate circumstances. The BRIC countries, particularly India and Brazil, have enacted import substitution as part of their developmental policies.

In India, Asian Paints started its operations in the pre-independence era, a time when India imported a wide variety of manufactured goods. But when World War II severely disrupted shipping routes, the opportunity for a new Indian paint manufacturing industry emerged. As imports declined, Asian Paints ramped up production and marketing of its products, one of the very few companies to take full advantage of the development. It has retained its number 1 market share in the fragmented domestic industry ever since.

Similarly, Russia's Furniture Maria capitalized on changing market conditions to expand a fledgling kitchen production business into a market leader. After a major supplier's default in 1998, an entire line of imported furniture completely disappeared from the market. Furniture Maria stepped in to fill the gap and since has become the country's main domestic kitchen supplier. The transition was not a seamless one. The company had to build and develop the skills of its management team, which consisted of childhood friends and senior top managers who had joined the firm at its inception in 1999. Over time, the business prospered even with new competition—success that company officials attributed to "our knowledge, experience, perhaps ambition, and a little luck."

It's important to note that the success of these rough diamonds didn't stem solely from these external political events. Serendipitous factors also allowed them to muster the resources they needed to produce these goods, and at a price to which the market would respond. They realized that the price differences between imported goods and their own products could work in their favor if they could exploit local sources, nurture local connections, and reduce operational costs. Such resources can help rough diamonds secure advantages in the long run, but establishing those connections takes time and considerable investment. Rough diamonds tackle that challenge with a relentless passion.

ROUGH DIAMONDS EXHIBIT RELENTLESS PASSION IN ADVERSITY

After dozens of interviews and months of research, we came to realize that rough diamonds perform as indigenous, or "zero-level," entrepreneurs. They serve as a wellspring of generative business activity, but there are still subtle yet important distinctions when comparing them with well-known entrepreneurs in the developed world. Unlike Bill Gates (Microsoft), Mark Zuckerberg (Facebook), and others who started their firms before they graduated from college, these indigenous entrepreneurs usually work for many years before venturing on their own.

Working experience is essential for entrepreneurial success in emerging markets for two reasons. First, unlike start-ups in developed countries that often sow the seeds of cutting-edge technology, entrepreneurial firms in emerging markets focus instead on entering a market niche that has not been well served. This has been particularly true among rough diamonds founded before the turn of the century. For executives in these firms, prior work experience afforded opportunities to study the market, assess changing demand and consumption patterns, nurture important local connections, and gain access to important resources. Second, unlike entrepreneurs in developed countries who might readily tap the resources of sophisticated equity and venture capital markets, rough diamonds have to muster resources on their own. While funds sometimes come from government sources, these firms typically rely on what they have at hand. This, of course, makes their instincts and the sharp entrepreneurial insights borne from deep experience all the more important.

Anatoliy Sedykh followed his instincts and experience and, like so many other rough diamonds, took an overlooked path and pursued it with a passion. He started down that road when he acquired several rundown, state-owned metallurgical companies at a low cost, cobbling them together to form Russia's OMK (United Metallurgical Company). His first years were dominated by the arduous work of integrating and renovating the companies, but he then started narrowing his focus on two potentially lucrative markets: railroad wheels and large-diameter pipes.

His co-owners and management team didn't like the idea of plunging into a nascent and untested market, but Anatoliy trusted his vision instead of relying solely on analytical studies. That determination won the day, and soon after, the company won a collection of critical long-term orders from Russian railroads and oil companies. While rough diamonds rely heavily on data and analyses, they don't allow themselves to be paralyzed or shy from bold moves because they're too busy overanalyzing the pros and cons. If seasoned intuition is undermined, very few entrepreneurs would emerge. Anatoliy balanced intuition and analysis, exemplifying both technological gravitas and sheer determination as he pursued his vision of a new manufacturing firm that would come of age during his lifetime.

As the history of OMK illustrates, rough diamond entrepreneurship is characterized by a notable level of irreverence—a vision of what should be without regard to the ensuing disruption of current business. At one time, local products in India were considered inferior to imported ones. Twenty-six years ago, virtually no one wanted anything made in India if they could find something else—whether it was a car, a computer, or piping and tubing. But the Sanghvi family of the Ratnamani Group didn't care about what was; it cared about what should be. They created a new vision for the firm, touting its piping and tubing as the "best in the world" for critical and high-end applications. Beyond that, they backed up their claims with highly innovative products that exceeded the expectations of their top customers. They didn't do it with any great fanfare. They just told people they had the best products and then produced the best products money could buy (box 3.2).

Box 3.2 Going About Your Business

Throughout our research, we found dozens of rough diamonds that avoided media attention as they built a foundation for their business. And despite their initial successes, they made a conscious decision to remain low key, away from the distracting elements of undue attention, until they had solidified that foundation.

Many of these rough diamonds said that sort of visibility would often attract envy and invite government oversight, which can distract from the company's focus. In China and Russia, in particular, newly found success triggers suspicions of illegal activity, the so-called original sin complex. Keeping out the media's notice reduced the chances of government intervention and investigation, especially early stages in the company's development. By the time these firms became large taxpayers and employed many individuals in the area, they were too big to fail in the eyes of local government.

At their early stages, they paid heed to the old Chinese proverb: "*men-sheng fa-da-cai*" (keep silent, make a big fortune). These rough diamonds eventually became more visible at a later stage of development, but early on, they took special care not to nurture the founder's ego. Instead, they reached out quietly to gather the resources they needed as they developed their business.

ROUGH DIAMONDS EXCEL AT BUILDING RELATIONSHIPS OR TECHNOLOGICAL EXPERTISE

As we studied the approaches rough diamonds took throughout their development, and especially during their early and middle stages, two distinct approaches stood out as vital to their growth and sustained success. The first was a core strategy focused on building the social contacts, business relationships, and extended networks that would benefit their firms. The second was a remarkable ability to acquire the technological expertise they needed to break into new markets and expand their business.

As relationship builders, the rough diamonds across the board excelled at nurturing contacts with a range of key stakeholders, from government contacts, to suppliers, to distributors. They often had little training in terms of technology and business expertise, but they more than compensated with their deep knowledge of connections and information channels in their societies and markets. A typical profile would reveal entrepreneurs who began working at an early age, but without much formal training. Along the way, they acquired the valuable social knowledge and personal skills they needed to survive in the local market. Over time they leveraged their expanding business sense and intuition with a natural ability to build key relationships, giving them the insights and connections to capitalize on emerging opportunities arising in a dynamic environment.

One such example was Jinkun Yu, the founder of KTK Group, a Chinese manufacturer of railway equipment. Yu might have left high school after the equivalent of his junior year, but his business record is exemplary. By the time he started KTK, he was forty-six years old and had already amassed years of experience as a salesperson in a plastic factory. As a factory manager at his prior job, Yu oversaw the production of the plastic coat hooks used in railway cars. From that vantage point, he saw the potential growth of the Chinese passenger railway network. At KTK, he turned that insight into a thriving business in an array of railway-related products, such as monitoring systems for the county's rail systems. Through his vast array of contacts and his personal skills, he crafted an embedded social network that helped him establish the firm as a specially designated provider for Chinese railway equipment. His once-small factory, now covering 200,000 square meters, has become a group with $600 million in fixed assets and some eighteen hundred employees.

Yu and other relationship-based leaders are especially good at managing their firms' relationships with the government. That many of them also hold the position of party branch secretary in their towns or villages is testimony to the importance of social bonding in the Chinese culture. The locally embedded personal backgrounds of these leaders helped ensure good government relationships. The ability to blend leadership roles in business, the broader industry, and key government associations is critical to success in the relationship-based, public-private blend of business in China.

The second approach to entrepreneurship stems from the acquisition of key technological expertise. While these technology-focused leaders often excel at building needed government relationships, they typically establish those relationships after their firms have achieved a certain measure of success. Instead, these technological entrepreneurs base their business from the start on their education and technical know-how. As they expand, they leverage their knowledge of a particular technology with local market knowledge to create advantages of scale and scope.

Anatoliy Sedykh already had an impressive educational and technical résumé when he launched OMK. He had received a PhD from the Moscow Institute of Steel and Alloys and had served as an economist at the Central Research Institute for the Iron and Steel Industry. By the time he launched OMK in 1992, he possessed more than enough technological expertise and entrepreneurial vision to push the company into products and markets that had not yet fully materialized for public consumption.

To be sure, in many cases such technological expertise develops as a company does. For example, the Indian firm Godawari Power & Ispat Ltd. (GPIL) produced its own innovation: a preheater for sponge iron kilns. Using natural gas as a primary reducing agent, GPIL's sponge-iron technology provided it with a more flexible and less capital-intensive method of production. Yet that innovation didn't come out of the clear blue sky; it was born of a constantly innovative mindset at its parent company, the Hira Group, and the Agrawal family that founded it. In fact, the Hira Group incorporated GPIL with an environmental innovation and a technological expertise.

Steel production generates prodigious amounts of heat. So GPIL was established not only as a steel plant but a power plant as well. It built a captive power plant with boilers fired by the waste heat thrown off by the steel production. The plant dramatically lowered the cost of power at the facility and helped the company build a reputation for ecological awareness. On its website, the company describes the factory as the "first one in the world to be registered with [the] CDM [clean development mechanism] Executive Board for entitlement of carbon credits under the Kyoto Protocol."

Keeping with its environmentally friendly philosophy, GPIL also has a twenty megawatt biomass power plant, which used rice husks as fuel for electricity generation. "Over the last few years," the website notes, "the company has scaled up its capacity fivefold and is today the third largest producer of coal based sponge iron in India."[2] And its vision, as proudly articulated by Abhishek Agrawal, the CEO of GPIL, says: "To become one of the most competitive integrated steel plants with entire value chain right from mining to finished steel with diversified products, contributing substantially in meeting consumers' needs, creating shareholder value and *pari passu* with powering India's growth to serve community and the nation in the decades to come."

Some companies benefit from the blend of technological expertise that multiple founders can bring to the table. WEG, a Brazilian manufacturer of motors and generators, was founded in 1961 by electrician Werner Ricardo Voigt, business administrator Eggon Joao da Silva, and mechanic Geraldo Werninghaus. Just as their first names lent an initial to the company name, each founder brought a different set of resources to the company. After military service, Voigt became one of the two selected soldiers to attend the Escola Técnica Federal, where he specialized in radiotelegraphy and electronics. Da Silva was a partner in a firm that produced exhaust pipes for vehicles. And Werninghaus started his career when he was fourteen years old in his father's workshop, where a universe of lathes, routers, grease, and cleansing wool rags quickly became part of his everyday life.

That combined commitment to various technological backgrounds comes through in its corporate culture. The company sums it up: "Since its foundation, WEG embraced the business strategy of building a highly qualified technical assistance network to develop customer reliance and to promote products, with the first technical assistants being accredited still in the 1960s."[3]

FIRST CAPITALIZE, THEN CREATE

As our research clearly indicated and these examples suggest, capitalizing on late development stood out as a requisite skill for rough diamonds in emerging markets. Changes in economic policies, market liberalization, government programs, globalization, and industry growth create risks, but they also offer rich opportunities for all firms. Rough diamonds not only identified emerging pockets of demand, not an easy chore itself, but they also had the acumen to aggressively enter these markets, displaying the best traits of entrepreneurship no matter where it's found.

These exemplary firms took a passionate approach to their business, which allowed them to pursue markets other companies avoided or overlooked. By capitalizing on their rich relationships, many of them gained access to critical resources and nurtured close connections with government, suppliers, and customers—all helping them develop responsive marketing programs. Others tapped into their deep technological expertise to innovate and, in many cases, create markets or advantages. Whereas the risks often overwhelm a regular firm, rough diamonds are able to balance risks with entrepreneurial savvy.

Identifying a market niche and moving toward it, however, marks just one step toward success. In emerging markets, demand might not be as viable or as consolidated as in developed economies even for the most promising products and services. Market inclusiveness and consolidation become critical requirements for success.

That is the subject of the next of the Four Cs.

4

Creating Inclusive Market Segments and Niches

2nd of 4 C's

why & for whom?

We created a need and space for [our] product offering. While we knew that India was still comfortable with mechanical watches, we gave our consumers a chance to upgrade and in turn changed the shape of the market we operated in. It was a risk, and we had the conviction that this had the potential of turning into a highly successful business proposition.

> —Bhaskar Bhat, Titan (an Indian rough diamond)

In emerging markets, demand is not only nascent, but it is typically situated in fragmented segments. Thus, even for established, maturing products...a successful marketing strategy is not confined to recognizing market opportunities, but also having to consolidate or pool fragmented pockets of demand into a viable market segment.

> —SKOLKOVO Business School–Ernst & Young Institute for Emerging Market Studies, *Rough Diamonds: The 4Cs Framework for Sustained High Performance*

Different approaches to building inclusive markets accentuate the core differences between rising companies in developed and emerging markets. The rough diamonds exhibit four primary traits: their responsiveness to new consumers'

47

...s, their ability to consolidate demand in previously
......market segments, their relentless effort at building
.....uation to boost their market positions, and their use of
timing or first-mover advantages to secure and build positions
ahead of erstwhile competitors.

The renowned management guru Peter Drucker once said
that the essence of any business is to "create a consumer."
In developed markets, companies work to generate a level
of demand that meets consumer needs and hits profit goals.
The usual study of consumer behavior focuses on demand
creation for existing or new products. Rough diamonds adopt
these fundamental marketing imperatives, of course, but their
circumstances also require that they develop new marketing
models in response to challenges that companies in developed
markets rarely face.

As we discussed in the preceding chapter, rough diamonds
excel at identifying often-overlooked market changes and taking action on those opportunities through their relationships
and technical expertise. The second of the Four Cs—creating
inclusive market niches and segments—becomes the natural
next marketing step to build off those bold initial moves.
However, this next step relies on a different set of skills.
Entrepreneurship is essential in the first stage. The second stage
requires a strong market orientation, focusing on consumers as
the primary sources of value creation.

In successfully narrowing their attention on the consumer,
the rough diamonds displayed four critical traits:

1. Responsiveness to new consumers' expectations

2. An ability to consolidate demand in previously unattended market segments and niches

3. A relentless effort to differentiate themselves in order to increase their market appeal

4. A keen sense of timing or a first-mover advantage that allows them to build and secure market share ahead of their competitors

Different companies leveraged these traits to different degrees, yet we found clear evidence of all four characteristics at work in the growth of every rough diamond.

ROUGH DIAMONDS ANTICIPATE AND RESPOND TO CONSUMER EXPECTATIONS

In order to serve a diverse customer base well, rough diamonds have to be customer oriented and attentive to changes in market demand, particularly current and anticipated changes in consumption patterns. They pay especially close attention to serving target clients, keeping communication channels open, and investing heavily in pre- and postsales services. Through this heightened level of customer responsiveness, rough diamonds develop an almost instinctual understanding of market trends, customer needs, and competitive forces.

Velkom, for example, responded to customer concerns about the quality of sausage to help build its market share in the Russian meat processing business. Founded by two men with deep expertise in the production process, extensive exposure to international markets, and an entrepreneurial zeal, Velkom quickly established itself as a force in the meat market. But its superior long-term performance through the 2000s stemmed from its deft market orientation. During that period, the company noted a subtle change in market trends: customers had gotten more skeptical about the quality and origin of sausage. Because the company was able to spot this trend early, it reorganized its services into small meat processing operations that catered exclusively to manufacturing premium products.

Velkom also boosted its marketing approach with a client-first value proposition, focusing on customers who sought diverse and unique tastes and had high expectations regarding quality, company responsiveness, and store aesthetics. After deliberating on various recipes and methods to increase quality, the company decided to reject soybeans and other genetically modified organism ingredients that consumers considered lower in quality. It narrowed its list of suppliers to work only with proven domestic and international companies. And all the while, it continued to interact with consumers to ensure it was making the right changes. Over time, the company became widely recognized for its strong consumer loyalty and trust. And while its early legacy was characterized by visionary entrepreneurship, the firm's responsiveness to a growing consumer segment ultimately became the hallmark of its success.

Beingmate took a similar approach to a market in which a company's reputation for quality is especially critical: infant foods and products. Hong Xie founded the Chinese firm in 1992, convinced of the market potential for domestically produced, high-quality infant products. He launched with a handful of products, including formula made from powdered milk, and started to establish quality as the core of Beingmate's culture. (In Chinese, Beingmate means, "the baby is beautiful because of love.") With its knowledge of the customs and practices of raising babies, Beingmate has built on a proven domestic formula by matching or exceeding international standards of quality. As we wrote this book, the company was one of the leading players in infant products and services in China.

A Systematic Approach

It's not enough to be responsive. Rough diamonds take a highly effective, systematic approach toward producing products that best match customer needs. They innovate, design, and draw from all their resources to establish excellence as marketers and producers. Thermax, a turbine and boiler manufacturer in India, has sustained more than 60 percent of its revenue from repeat customers, thanks largely to its customer-centric approach. Its corporate philosophy, "Improving your business is our business," reflects how the company differentiates itself by focusing on the value it adds for its customers' businesses. It supplements that value proposition with an operating flexibility and systematic processes that ensure its products are designed from the start to be business friendly for customers. The company has a well-earned reputation as a solution provider in the industrial energy and environment space.

In Brazil, three enterprising brothers—Luiz Eugenio, José Antonio, and Wilson Donizetti Bassi—launched Açotubo from scratch. They started producing steel disks from sheets that Caterpillar sold as scrap. Step by step, the brothers built on this line of business, expanding their operations, consolidating partnerships, and forging distribution channels. As they ramped up the business and its operations, their cost structure allowed them to provide increasingly competitive prices. The biggest shot in the arm came when they differentiated their offerings by launching a rapid delivery service, pledging deliveries within twenty-four hours for customers in a 200 kilometer radius. In recent years, it has posted a growth rate of about 30 percent, and it projects revenue of 1 billion Brazilian reals ($588.2 million) for 2012.

Anticipating New Customer Demand

Rough diamonds not only recognize new markets; they recognize the evolving niches within those markets and capitalize on them. While working abroad, Sergei Plastinin recognized the potential for a new concentrate while traveling abroad, so he brought the idea back and put it to work at WBD Beverages (Vimm-Bill-Dann Napitki) in Russia. Not only was the concentrate quite flavorful, he realized; it was potentially more economical because it was barely one-sixth the size of ready-made juice and therefore convenient to store and less expensive to transport. That insight gave birth to a new market for Russia, juice bottling, that became a high-growth industry in the country.

Some rough diamonds recognize a new technological twist that could build a new market for an old product. India's long-standing leader in watches and timepieces, Titan, is on the constant lookout for unexplored market segments. It found one with the introduction of quartz technology for wristwatches. Although quartz technology was well accepted globally, the Indian watch market remained comfortable with mechanical watches. The move to quartz would require a radical market transformation and a big leap of faith by Titan. So the company crafted an exceptionally good watch design, branding strategy, and local distribution network. "We created a need and space for [our] product offering," said Bhaskar Bhat, the company's managing director. "While we knew that India was still comfortable with mechanical watches, we gave our consumers a chance to upgrade and in turn changed the shape of the market we operated in. It was a risk, and we had the conviction that this had the potential of turning into a highly successful business proposition.''

ROUGH DIAMONDS CONSOLIDATE
FRAGMENTED POCKETS
OF DEMAND

Demand in emerging markets is not only nascent; it's often very fragmented. Even for established products such as beverages and health products, a successful marketing strategy has to go beyond recognizing market opportunities: it has to extend to strategies that consolidate the splintered pockets of demand into a viable market segment. To be sure, demand consolidation occurs in developed countries as well, but the problem is much more pronounced in emerging and developing economies because of their fledgling market institutions.[1] Add to that the mix of international influences and domestic variation, such as the broad geographical stretch of Russia and the many languages, cultures, and castes in India, and efforts to harmonize consumer demand through a standard product or service become exceedingly important.

These consolidation activities can occur in multiple phases of a firm's growth curve. It can happen at the embryonic stage, for example, drawing on insight when demand is difficult to track and early market leaders have staked out a broader position. It can happen in the aftermath of a market shake-up as marginal or inefficient firms are weeded out, opening up opportunities for entry into emerging market niches by stronger and more resilient rough diamonds. Even as the markets mature, industry incumbents begin to reap benefits from lower costs and larger volumes and are less disposed to challenge these rising firms.

FIGURE 4.1 Phases of Creating Inclusive Market Growth

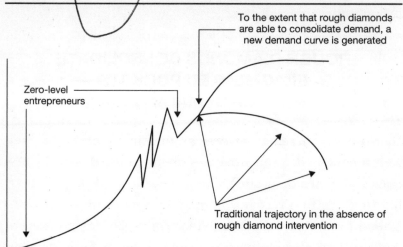

To the extent that rough diamonds are able to consolidate demand, a new demand curve is generated

Zero-level entrepreneurs

Traditional trajectory in the absence of rough diamond intervention

Embryonic　Growth　"Shakeout"　Leveling/Maturation　Decline　Regeneration

Note: Creating inclusive market niches can occur in two phases: at the embryonic stage or following a shakeout arising from industry maturation or a government regulation. In both cases, an RD has to aggregate fragmented pockets of demand into a larger and viable market segment.

To the extent that rough diamonds build on success, they can delay the maturity of some products or regenerate an entirely new product cycle (figure 4.1). Delaying maturity is not altogether novel, of course. Sony used this strategy in Japan in the 1970s, creating new features for radios and other maturing products. Our research showed that unlike Sony and other Japanese companies that initiated product embellishments as a part of their overall marketing strategies, companies that weren't market leaders could capitalize on these same strategies. Rough diamonds did exactly that.

This delay of maturation doesn't always have to happen on the surface or in simple product-level innovation. In India, Bombay Rayon Fashions put an innovative spin on its already mature system for ordering seasonal garments. Because of the difficulty in forecasting demand in the industry, garment buyers would typically place small orders according to seasonal trends. For Bombay Rayon, however, small demand didn't suffice for building a profitable, large-scale operation, so the company developed a design team to analyze trends and consumption patterns. Armed with that insight, the company could introduce multiple small batches of designs that met varied customer preferences while still providing the scale necessary for the company to remain profitable over time.

Consolidating Around the Brand

Godrej Consumer Products in India employed another tactic often used by rough diamonds: consolidating a niche by aggressively building the brand. Godrej has invested heavily in its brand over the years, building a reputation for quality and trustworthiness, and that brand image has become one of its biggest competitive advantages. Its reputation makes a huge difference to both consumers and distributors. As the Indian market develops and becomes increasingly complex, the company believes consumers confused by multiple options will gravitate toward a brand name with a strong reputation.

To make sure it maintains that brand reputation, Godrej begins by developing a deep understanding of local consumers and then tailoring products and services for specific consumer segments. It's a method that works in India, company officials said, but it would work in any other market predisposed to strong local brands. The proximity to and interactions with local consumers provide a sustainable foundation for product differentiation, and it enhances the company's ability to develop robust distribution channels, particularly in India, where direct availability is considered a core competency. The bond that ties all of those competencies together is Godrej's impeccable brand.

Consolidation Through Product Portfolio Adjustments

In Russia as much as anywhere else, rough diamonds have pieced together the right mix of products to address customer needs and coalesce a fragmented market. WBD Beverages implemented a brand management system that brings its multiple beverage brands under one umbrella. Under that arrangement, it can centrally coordinate its different brands of juices and nectars, from the low, middle, and high prices designed to target its various consumer profiles. OZNA structured its internal product development efforts so it can evolve with the technological changes in the broader oil-and-gas industry, a strategy embodied in its company slogan: "Accompanying oil and gas producers."

Slavyanka Plyus can quickly adjust its portfolio of confectionary goods by taking advantage of its remarkable production and distribution networks. Its advanced product lines allow the company to reach a broad cross-section of the population, including most of the market's various social niches. It backs that market coverage with an equally extensive reach, opening distribution centers and establishing a dealer network throughout the Russian Federation. Its formal distributor status ensures priority rights to discounted products in assigned territories, order fulfillment priority, participation in additional discounting programs, and a range of consulting, advertising, and information support.

Phased Expansion

Companies can also coalesce market fragments through a deliberate and thoughtful approach to expansion over time. In 1926, two Italian immigrants in Brazil, Costabile and Giancola

Matarazzo, decided they didn't want to import their hunting weapons or ammunition, so they launched CBC Cartucho and started manufacturing their own in São Paulo. Their factory grew large enough to supply products to local troops during the Constitutionist Revolution in 1932. But what distinguished this company from its competitors—and what started to pull together several distinct markets—was its decision to expand overseas as early as 1936. It eventually entered thirty-four countries, giving it the scale it needed to take advantage of the highly oligarchical nature of the arms industry. Through its contracts with the government, which preferred to work with a small number of suppliers, CBC Cartucho slowly built its reputation and quality and became one of the major suppliers of ammunition to the North Atlantic Treaty Organization, police forces, and hunting aficionados around the world. It now sells products in seventy countries.

Internally, it complemented that growth with a foundation of innovation, product improvements, and human resource development. To ensure safety and quality, the company maintains a ballistic laboratory with sophisticated and advanced technologies. It developed a fully integrated production system, complete with an industrial park that houses the powder, ammunition, and mixture factories. And with its Talentos de Caliber development program, it has institutionalized a system for training current and local managers to sustain its growth over the long term.

ROUGH DIAMONDS DEVELOP DEEP DIFFERENTIATION ADVANTAGES

For years, Brazil's appliance manufacturers offered mostly standard products at low prices. They paid little attention to special features, such as ice dispensers in refrigerator doors, and the mass-market strategy worked well because of the relatively small Brazilian middle class. As the middle class began to expand, however, demand for more features in appliances opened up new opportunities.

Enter Esmaltec, Brazilian manufacturer of kitchen and domestic appliances. While other competitors waited for the middle-class segment to grow, Esmaltec seized this opportunity to build ahead of demand and differentiate its appliances by offering the affordable product features its focused market segment wanted. Two-door refrigerators might not seem to be cutting edge in Europe or North America, but in Brazil, those features had a widespread appeal for many lower- to middle-class families. Esmaltec changed production from one-door to two-door refrigerators, added its frost-free technology, and did it all without a large increase in price. For consumers, it was a winning formula: more features at relatively the same prices. Esmaltec used its early market advantage to innovate and lower the energy consumption of all its products, further enhancing its value proposition.

By offering these new product features, the company established a clear differentiation advantage and consolidated that market position with its affordable prices, putting it and its consumers in a win-win position. Essentially the company has protected itself from competitors that try to fight back with aggressive prices. Because of its differentiation, the firm can offer products at premium prices or prices that consumers are willing to pay.

Of course, this can be a herculean task for late entrants to markets where more established firms, foreign multinationals in particular, have already been offering higher-priced, differentiated products. To challenge these industry leaders entails a sizable marketing investment and resources that few small companies can afford. The challenge is to provide products of similar quality at a much lower price than foreign firms do. That can be exceedingly difficult, but rough diamonds have one distinct advantage: they know the local markets better than foreign competitors do and use that knowledge to tailor their products to meet specific local needs, as Esmaltec did when it started offering new amenities to its appliances.

Simply knowing the specialized local conditions is not a guarantee of success. To succeed, a firm has to formulate a unique way of connecting with its targeted segment that reflects this deep understanding of local needs and preferences. Natura used its local insights to differentiate its products and consolidate its position in a market niche for cosmetics, fragrances, and hygiene products. By the time the firm was founded in 1969, the Brazilian cosmetic market had been established for years and was approaching early maturity. Differentiation in these later market development stages has proved difficult because the existing rules of the game favored cost-price reductions, not differentiation. In order to set itself apart, Natura needed a radically bold idea.

It came up with a marketing strategy that considers beauty as an instinctive aspiration of every human being and free of preconceived ideas and contrivances. Beauty, it believes, is natural. On the product side, Natura acquired advanced methods of plant hormone extraction from L'Oréal, a technology that delivered two distinct benefits: a natural sense of beauty in its products and brand image and a lower-cost method of production that increased productivity. By unleashing the combination of a new natural concept and its new technology, Natura delayed the full maturation of beauty products into commodities. That created the foundation for future brands in later stages of the firm's development and, more important, consolidated a new market niche that Natura still dominates.

The nature of emerging economies makes differentiation a challenge because it occurs in markets still advancing through maturation. In many cases, consumers might not view differentiation as an advantage, preferring instead to purchase items at the lowest price (i.e., commodity-based pricing). Marico, an Indian firm in the beauty and wellness sector, overcame this challenge by transforming a traditionally commodity-driven business into a branded consumer goods business. Creating differentiation when consumers are already predisposed to a maturing product can be daunting, but Harsh Mariwala, Marico's founder and chairman, initiated an innovative packaging idea. His "think small" campaign set out to fulfill the unmet consumer demand for small, portable containers that could be bought at affordable prices from any small retail outlet. This bold but fresh idea transformed the company's public image and solidified its brand and its differentiation strategy. The company continues to take advantage of opportunities by transforming its brands, its products, and the marketplace. "Success, for me, is in identifying spaces where one can be a market leader," Mariwala said. "Our endeavor is to seek blue ocean spaces—those untapped markets where our strategies can reap the maximum growth dividends. Finding niches, while side-stepping heavily crowded markets, has been a key driver of our sustained success."

Products in different phases of their life cycles can pose headaches for companies trying to differentiate themselves through a unique mix of offerings. Slavyanka Plyus, the Russian confectionary, produced a wide range of products to suit the varied income levels of its consumers. In order to sustain this type of differentiation, however, it had to revamp its entire production system, adding new technologies to fully automate its process. The upgrade produced most of the expected benefits, such as ensuring increased annual output, but it also ensured that the firm could deliver across all its niche markets. It now works at constantly improving the formulation of its products and implementing new technologies that give the company the flexibility to produce more targeted products, including premium products made with healthier ingredients.

Such success is not limited to consumer goods. Rough diamonds in heavy industry excel in customer service as a differentiating factor as well. Two Indian firms, Lakshmi Machine Works and Sudhir Gensets, implemented innovative after-sales service programs, an important source of competitive advantage because their products play critical roles in their customers' operations. Lakshmi, which produces equipment for textile factories, built a reputation of consistent value by bundling its machines with different value-added services. The after-sales relationships deepened that brand image.

Sudhir Gensets, a power supply systems maker, established itself three decades ago when small and medium businesses in India faced a severe electricity shortage. Sudhir Seth, chairman and managing director, saw this as a long-term opportunity; in fact, energy shortages still plague many Indian businesses today. Sudhir Gensets now has more than forty thousand customers across India, and it has increased its market share to more than 5 percent in the Punjab area after changing its sales-oriented approach to a service-based, customer-oriented approach.

ROUGH DIAMONDS GRAB THE FIRST-MOVER ADVANTAGE

Timing, they say, is everything. Rough diamonds regularly stake out market position by moving first, and quickly, to consolidate their advantage.[2] Typically first movers are innovators who enter a market before anyone else. Rough diamonds tend to take a slightly different approach, using their nimbleness and flexibility to move into open niches or segments that competitors have abandoned. So while conventional theories associate first movers with firms that pioneer new markets, rough diamonds tend to be the first to take advantage of new opportunities in existing markets.

In the 1950s, Brazil was enjoying rapid economic growth, and many industries introduced new equipment to help satisfy the need for heightened manufacturing capacity. But no companies were producing the replacement parts needed when that equipment inevitably broke down. Cinpal jumped on the opportunity in 1950, launching itself as Brazil's only domestic manufacturer of forged and cast parts for cars and machinery. It quickly started producing parts and components for trucks, buses, agricultural and industrial tractors, and passenger cars. In 1973, it began manufacturing parts for mining industry equipment. Its reputation as one of the first companies to produce spare parts in Brazil earned it a formidable advantage that it retains today.

Sitronics Telecom underpinned its first-mover advantage in Russia with an early commitment to technological innovation. Now a market leader in information technology, telecommunications, and microelectronics, the company obtained its initial knowledge and expertise about developments from Czech company Strom Telecom. After extensively studying the industry's technology, it leveraged this expertise to an advantage that competitors could not match. The company cites many reasons for its ability to stay ahead of competitors from a dedication to automated business processes, to an incentive program for engineers, and to regular investments in development and well-timed initial public offerings. But chief among those reasons are its ability to expand quickly and replicate its business solutions in new regions and its openness to change, innovation, and development.

Virtually every rough diamond in India can tell a story of its first-mover advantage. For example:

(3) • The Amtek Group created Amtek India in 1982 to seize on the young but growing automobile industry in that country.

(4) • Indian-made tubular products were not exactly the first preference among customers some twenty-six years ago, but Ratnamani Metals & Tubes jumped into the market with applications for a diverse set of industries. It started by targeting companies that used foreign-made stainless steel tubes and pipes for general applications and then moved up the value chain to higher-value applications. (an initial existence)

(5) • The Indian aluminum industry remains in a nascent stage, but Parekh Aluminex has continued to grow since it started producing aluminum packaging in 1994.

As the sustained success of all these rough diamonds show, the ability to identify market niches and enter them, while a necessary first step, does not fully explain the success these companies have posted in their emerging markets. In addition to consolidating demand in previously fragmented markets and building core competencies, rough diamonds exploit a multitude of methods—from well-timed moves on open market segments to well-planned differentiation strategies—to consolidate markets and increase their advantages.

This market-oriented leadership serves rough diamonds well, but sustained success requires a keen and constant attention on internal operations as well. Without securing and constantly seeking to expand the cost advantages they've earned, companies will not be able to sustain their advantages. As the rough diamonds show, the next step is to move from demand to supply considerations. And that is the focus of the third of the Four Cs.

5

Crafting Operational Excellence

RDs [rough diamonds] regard agility as an innate skill, much like a "gene" in their embedded organizational systems. Failure to respond quickly might result in an opportunity being transformed into a threat. [Chinese] RDs regard such opportunities as the basis for responding quickly to changes.

> —SKOLKOVO Business School–Ernst & Young Institute for Emerging Market Studies, *Rough Diamonds: The 4Cs Framework for Sustained High Performance*

While it is true that emerging markets tend to have lower labor costs, it is unlikely that these alone will lead to successful applications. In this study, operational excellence is realized in a number of diverse ways, and other factors beyond low costs are critical to establishing a low-cost leadership position.

> —SKOLKOVO Business School–Ernst & Young Institute for Emerging Market Studies, *Rough Diamonds: The 4Cs Framework for Sustained High Performance*

Operational excellence is the kernel of business excellence—the pivotal factor that determines whether rough diamonds are able to attain the next stage of sustained performance. Excellence does not derive from a magic formula but through an array of strategies and activities, including integrated logistics and supply chain management; collaborative innovation; whole system quality assurance; and flexible, agile, and cohesive management systems.

The first two of the Four Cs look at rough diamond excellence from the demand perspective—the ways in which these firms have sustained profitable growth through tapping into market dynamics. But no company can thrive over the long haul if it doesn't also excel at the internal operational demands of its business. So we turn to the supply side and the ways rough diamonds craft operational excellence.

Across all the rough diamonds we studied, leaders repeatedly stressed the importance of efficient and flexible operations as a key to sustaining their exemplary performance over time. While the particulars of those internally focused strategies varied from company to company, these companies exhibited four overarching core competencies as a whole: they integrated and optimized their logistics and supply chain management, took a collaborative approach to innovation, stressed a whole-system approach to quality assurance, and built management systems that were flexible, agile and cohesive.

ROUGH DIAMONDS EXCEL AT INTEGRATED LOGISTICS AND SUPPLY CHAIN MANAGEMENT

Managing inbound and outbound logistics is particularly challenging in an emerging economy. Like demand in these markets, the logistical ecosystem is fragmented, and the underlying infrastructure supporting it is hardly adequate. This makes the supply chain that connects suppliers, producers, and customers particularly vulnerable to delays, disruptions, and sometimes outright cancellations. Worse yet, this lack of integrated coordination creates uncertainty and poor information, which heightens transaction costs.

Supply chain management becomes a critical managerial challenge for companies in emerging markets. Rough diamonds nurture their relationships with all parties and partners to ensure a proper structure for transactions and exchanges. Of course, building efficient supply chain systems requires investments in both financial and human capital. Establishing that in an emerging market is not for the faint of heart, but decisions involving significant capital investments rarely are. And yet most rough diamonds from the BRIC countries had to invest heavily in both backward and forward integration, often building out the complete supply chain on their own. Even as they build scale in the marketplace, they promote their own sales networks and collaborate closely with distributors to ensure their products get to customers as promised (box 5.1).

Every rough diamond has gone through this process to a greater or lesser extent. In Brazil, for example, Magnesita developed an integrated value chain from scratch, establishing a network that stretched from mining, to the manufacturing of nonclay refractory products, and to distribution and logistics. The company took a more vertical approach to the business largely because it needed to maintain reliable links across so many critical phases of the supply chain. The price of key raw materials, for example, accounts for 45 percent of the production cost in the refractory business. Moreover, the quality of those raw materials largely dictates the quality of the final product. So in order to control the supply of raw materials, the company has established eighty-five active mining concessions with extensive mineral reserves. Through this backward

Box 5.1 Jinglong's Operational Excellence

The operational excellence of Jinglong, a Chinese manufacturer of solar grade, solar cell, and semiconductor device grade silicon products, grew out of three key events during its inception. It was one of the first companies to capitalize monocrystalline silicon technology, a single-crystal silicon base that was developed at Hebei Industry University in 1995. "The research achievement from college laid the foundation of the firm to a large extent," said Jianbo Xu, the assistant president of Jingao Solar Ltd., a Jinglong subsidiary. The company received a second boost when it forged a joint venture with Japan's Songgong Semiconductor Ltd. That enabled the company, which knew it had a captive market, to produce on a large scale. "Songgong's capital and technology is the catalyst of our development," Xu said. And third, the company's promoter, Baofang Jin, was not only a legendary entrepreneur but also a strong political figure. His solid government background led to critical policy and fiscal support and the trust of a foreign investor.

With these supportive developments, Jinglong eschewed small investments, choosing instead to invest and develop the entire industrial chain. That decision had two overarching pillars: the vertical, from crystal pulling to ingot cutting to wafer slicing and to solar cell producing; and the horizontal, from monocrystalline, to polycrystalline, to packaging. While competitors found the strategy risky and avoided the market, Jinglong capitalized on its early success and experience. "We should expand along the chain of monocrystalline and polycrystalline silicon industry," Xu said. "We never cut our investment . . . because of a bad market condition." Jinglong now produces at a scale that maintains consistent quality at the lowest cost in the industry. Said Xu, "We are trying to be the largest supplier of monocrystalline solar power battery chips."

integration, the firm has access to high-quality raw materials at lower costs than its competitors, limiting its exposure to price volatility. In 2010, it sourced 70 percent of its raw material needs from its own operations in Brazil, the United States, Europe, and China.

In terms of logistics, Magnesita also opted to locate close to its primary clients and suppliers. It sits an average distance of 435 kilometers from its clients and 529 kilometers from its main suppliers. And to increase its efficiency, the company uses Ferrovia Centro Atlantica railway operated by CVRD (Companhia Vale do Rio Doce) to transport its products internally and to port. As we wrote this book, the port did not yet operate at full capacity, so Magnesita had even greater logistical latitude to expand its mineral and refractory exports volume if needed.

Godawari Power & Ispat Ltd., the integrated steel manufacturer we introduced in chapter 3, started out as a steel manufacturer but vertically integrated to reduce its costs. In 2004, it began to integrate back into the mining business by acquiring licenses from the Ministry of Mines for iron ore extraction at the Borio Tibbu and Ari Dongri area in Chhattisgarh, both of which hold high-grade reserves. The company also built a 73 megawatt, on-site power plant that produces enough energy to power the entire factory. And because it uses waste heat captured from the sponge iron manufacturing process, the generating station allowed substantial reductions in fuel costs. Today the firm has traversed the entire value chain, becoming an end-to-end manufacturer of steel wires and one of the lowest-cost producers in the industry.

Jinluo Group built an impressive sales distribution channel to support its packaged food and meat productions. It scaled up its sales network throughout China, building out to forty-two sales offices, more than thirty-three hundred franchise shops, and more than nine thousand authorized dealers. In cities, Jinluo puts salespeople directly in supermarkets to interact with customers and promote sales. In rural areas, the products are sold through a network of franchise outlets. Using a primarily direct sales approach, the firm makes sure that its products can be delivered to consumers in the fastest and safest way. Underpinning all this, Jinluo set up an advanced e-business system through which its chain of stores can inquire about products, order online, and have their purchases distributed automatically.

Another company in the food processing industry, this one in Brazil, increased its market share by expanding its partnerships in phases. Coniexpress focused its sales first on small- and medium-sized networks rather than beating on the doors of large retailers such as Carrefour. Using this incremental scale-up strategy, the firm put together a team of independent sales representatives in 150 offices that reach the entire country. By 1995, 70 percent of its revenue came from its small- and medium-business partners. After ensuring sales to smaller stores, the firm gradually began to turn its attention to the major retailers.

ROUGH DIAMONDS NURTURE COLLABORATIVE INNOVATION

The stereotype suggests that manufacturing firms in emerging markets excel solely because they have lower labor costs. But labor cost accounts for just one part of the entire value chain. Although it is true that many of these firms start as a labor-intensive business with little added value—they are at the bottom of the industrial value chain—the companies that sustain their success have recognized the need to move up the value chain in order to establish a comprehensive approach to cost-efficiency. Yet as the rough diamonds show, cost reductions alone do not lead to sustained advantages. Such firms must innovate as well, and to achieve that goal, they need to implement a learning process that generates new ideas or builds the resources to develop or acquire the innovation they need.

Rough diamonds inevitably adopt a collaborative approach to innovation, often building up their R&D capabilities through heavy investments in education, hiring top researchers, and creating focused learning centers. Like most other companies, the rough diamonds readily partner with other firms, but they stand apart from the also-rans because of the pace at which they learn from others. Many of them have built active alliances with foreign companies and universities, quickly gleaning new competencies, internalizing process improvements, and even developing new technologies—all despite coming in as late entrants to the game (box 5.2).

Box 5.2 Collaborative Learning at Thermax

Thermax, an Indian manufacturer in the turbine and boiler business, managed the innovation challenge by fusing long-term technological partnerships, nurturing indigenous innovation, and continuously improving product quality. Given the technical nature of its business, the firm spent more than 16 million euros (more than $20 million) to establish its own R&D center soon after it launched. It upgraded and expanded its innovation capacity when it set up the ambitious new Research, Technology, and Innovation Centre in Pune that focused on five centers of excellence critical to its industry: combustion and gasification, heat transfer, material science, solar, and biotechnology.

Along with its indigenous innovation capabilities, the company has been effective in sourcing and learning cutting-edge knowledge from global technology leaders, including Babcock & Wilcox (United States), Kawasaki Thermal Engineering Company (Japan), Eco Tech (Canada), Honeywell (United States), Bloom Engineering (Germany), and Struthers Wells and Ozone Systems (United States). Each year it executes on a technology absorption plan to fully integrate and internalize these imported technologies. Its innovation has established Thermax as a market leader, and it has earned awards for its R&D team's performance, including the National Award at ACREX (Air Conditioning, Refrigeration, & Building Service Exhibition) for the design of Trigenie, a chiller that works on exhaust gas and other sources of heat, and the top prize for the most innovative product design at the Bry-Air Awards.

Chinese rough diamonds have done an especially good job of learning from partnerships with universities and foreign firms. The Qinghua Group, for example, cooperates with foreign companies to learn from them. In 2000, it improved its technological standards by partnering with the Korean company POSCO and the Japanese company Asahi Glass. The same collaborative innovation mind-set serves as a key strategy for many of China's high-tech companies, including Jinglong, the solar cell manufacturer. First, the company spent 6 percent of its annual revenue on R&D, a relatively large amount for an embryonic firm. Second, it collaborated with universities and institutions in China, the United States, the Netherlands, and Australia to develop new technologies. And third, it invested 150 million RMB ($24 million) to set up a research complex with a technology center, three R&D centers, two labs, and two postdoctoral workstations. Moreover, the firm held seminars regularly and sent employees to Japan and Switzerland to receive training.

The results speak for themselves. Jinglong finished over six hundred innovation projects since its inception in 1996, and it is the only company in Hebei Province to make the National Technology Innovation Pilot Enterprises list. Its subsidiary Jing'Ao successfully implemented a program that produced the first solar battery in the world to reach a photoelectric transformation efficiency rate of 18.9 percent.

True collaborative innovation requires a deep commitment to an integrated organizational process and structure. Research and development groups have to work closely with other business units, including marketing and sales departments, that can help keep innovation oriented to customers. The exchange of information among these various parties can occur sequentially or reciprocally, depending on the objectives. Natura, whose natural beauty products we discussed in the previous chapter, established a fruitful balance of sequential and reciprocal learning. In sequential terms, the company built up its R&D expertise through a series of moves, starting with the acquisition of technology from L'Oréal. It then supplemented that expertise with its own investment in innovation capacity: R&D expenses accounted for about 4.2 percent of sales income in 2005, 6.7 percent in 2007, and 7.8 percent in 2010, according to the company's annual report. A portion of that money funds a research center and pays a collection of scientists from well-regarded Brazilian institutions. To encourage continued innovation, the company rewards researchers for important achievements in their fields.

Building on that, Natura established a process for reciprocal learning, tying marketing and other customer-facing departments with its R&D teams. Natura conducts market research before starting any project, and it develops only products that fit market demands and support the core brand concept. Mamãe e Bebê—Mother and Baby—was one of those products. Since babies first experience "fundamental love" with their mother during pregnancy, the company developed this product line with an eye toward strengthening this natural and special bond. All of the products in this collection have been designed to enhance the daily care of both mother and child by awakening all five senses. And in another example of reciprocal innovation at work, the Mamãe e Bebê products are developed in close cooperation with pediatricians and dermatologists.

ROUGH DIAMONDS EMBRACE TOTAL QUALITY ASSURANCE

In emerging economies, where weak institutions lack a consistent enforcement power, sustained success depends largely on a firm's reputation for high-quality products, services, and relationships. The ineffectual government institutions—regulatory, judicial, and otherwise—allow companies and individuals to break contracts with ease, costing businesses in emerging markets untold millions of dollars each year. Trust in business transactions plummets.

Simply put, delivering quality products and services builds trust. Rough diamonds understand this, and they make every effort possible to deliver the highest quality lest their images suffer and their costs increase. By ensuring quality along the entire value chain, the goods that rough diamonds produce regularly earn national and international quality accreditations. The rough diamonds in Russia have built a solid reputation with a consistent and high-level commitment to quality improvement across all their operations. Most of those firms maintain a high-level ISO quality certification, but MLVZ is the only company in its region with a Passport of High Quality Enterprise issued by the Russian quality control agency.

WBD Beverages and other rough diamonds in the country's food processing sector deservedly promote their track record of high quality, whereas their competitors often have to recall products or defend legal claims due to poor-quality products. "A quality management system enables us to reach a new level of operation through higher customer satisfaction, market competitiveness, and improved position in a rapidly changing market," said Vladimir G. Borisov, marketing director at Mordovtsement, a cement manufacturer. "Our quality certification assures consumers that they are dealing with a company that has a modern material-technical base and skills and conforms to international standards."

As we noted earlier, Velkom boosted consumer demand by producing high-quality sausage, but it could accomplish and sustain that improvement only with an obsessive control over the quality of all its inputs and outputs. The company uses modern equipment, and all technical procedures, from slaughtering to packaging, are strictly followed. Velkom was the first company in its industry to introduce an enterprise resource system to increase efficiency and quality controls on a corporate scale. It pioneered the introduction of a hazard identification process to ensure better safety at its facilities. And it adopted the Quantitative Ingredients Declaration, which requires a detailed disclosure of ingredients.

A chain is only as strong as its weakest link, and a company's commitment to quality is only as strong as its point of lowest quality control. The Anhui Yingliu Group took that commitment to heart. Like many other rough diamonds, this Chinese manufacturer of mechanical parts and castings has earned most of the top national and international accreditations, including ISO 9001. But the firm also created an independent quality department in each of its subsidiaries, giving them the sole responsibility of strengthening the quality of the links at every stage of its operations. Some 220 employees work directly for these departments. Its obsession with quality helped the Yingliu Group build an impeccable reputation for business and built trust with partners and customers.

In India, rough diamonds have guiding principles for quality management embedded in their corporate values and cultures. Because stainless steel tubes are critical to the performance of related industries that require high quality and reliability, Ratnamani built its competitiveness in this sector through a corporate-wide commitment to quality management. This program not only monitors the manufacturing processes but also holds workers strictly accountable for product quality (box 5.3).

Box 5.3 Vijai Electricals' Quality Control

Since its inception, Vijai Electricals' strategy has focused on maintaining the highest standards of quality control and assurance as challenging customer needs emerged. It uses the best materials, optimized design, and effective processes to maintain high quality in the design, manufacture, and supply of its customized power transmission and distribution equipment. A key aspect of its quality management lies in its cross-functional collaboration designed to produce maximum quality improvement. This integration effort across a range of company operations can happen because the company committed itself to a management system and culture that makes quality the prime responsibility for every employee. Vijai Electricals' quality commitment has been recognized by accreditations from prominent international quality agencies.

ROUGH DIAMONDS BUILD FLEXIBLE, AGILE, AND COHESIVE MANAGEMENT SYSTEMS

Unlike developed countries, which tend to have formal institutions that enact and enforce laws on property rights and social welfare systems, emerging markets have yet to develop robust safeguards for property and well-being. Instead, their institutions are best described as informal and reliant primarily on existing conventions, customs, cultural mores, and norms.[1] This puts a heavy premium on relationships in both daily life and business transactions. Close business relationships are imperative to building trust. Holistically managing those relationships—from the individual, to the partner company, to the entire value chain network—ranks among the highest priorities of business in emerging markets.

The rough diamonds in these markets consider employees a key business asset—in many cases, more valuable than capital or technology. And because emerging markets tend to have a large supply of mobile, low-skilled workers and a short supply of senior managers, motivating, training, and retaining employees becomes one of the most critical strategies underlying the sustained success of these firms.

In our analysis, the management systems adopted by rough diamonds—in some cases, during periods of adversity—tend to have three distinctive characteristics: flexibility, agility, and cohesion. These characteristics are underpinned by strong and supportive structures, risk taking, and resilient corporate cultures that lead to enduring employee commitment and loyalty.

Flexibility

The stereotyped depictions of Russian management systems tend to accentuate their rigid, authoritative, and centralized structures, yet rough diamonds in Russia have done an exceptional job of combining a unitary leadership structure with processes that generate deep loyalty and commitment, a combination that helps breed flexibility and success. Many of the people we interviewed noted that the Russian rough diamonds are different from other private companies in the country because of these distinctively pliable managerial systems, which are almost as good as any leading company in the West. In our analyses, their management systems, along with attendant components, ranked as the most important explanation for their success (box 5.4).

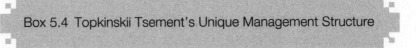

Box 5.4 Topkinskii Tsement's Unique Management Structure

By the time Topkinskyi Tsement, a leader in the cement industry, joined a holding company, it had become an internal management training school for other subsidiaries in the company. Its CEOs systematically rotated to other subsidiaries every two or three years in order to share their advanced managerial expertise with other units. In contrast to the traditional Russian system of tightly controlled bureaucracy with an elite, Russian rough diamonds place a high emphasis on openness and individual development, an approach that makes them receptive to creative ideas and responsive to market changes.

Given that most of the rough diamonds based in Russia operate in the consumer goods sector, subject to the whims of the consumer market, flexible decision-making systems allow them to quickly adapt internally to changes in the external marketplace. Over the past decade, for example, many of the country's consumer sectors went through significant consolidation. That ushered in intense market competition, and adaptability to those changes differentiated the high-performing firms from the rest. MLVZ reorganized its plant and joined the Sinergia Group, which supplied greater access to detailed information about market trends that affected the entire group's supply chain management system. Today that flexibility has become a hallmark of Russia's rough diamonds. "The strength of our company lies in the ability to quickly respond to market threats and opportunities," said Raisa Vasilevna Demina, general director of Velkom. "We do not hesitate to review the basic assumptions in our operations."

These strong yet pliable management systems tend to grow out of a strong supporting structure and strong processes. We encountered numerous examples of this throughout our research, enough to write several books. These two cases, however, offer a glimpse into two facets of these supportive structures that help illustrate the essence of flexible management systems:

- In terms of decision-making processes, Godrej Consumer Products has a flat, nonhierarchical operating environment. Because the company focuses on four categories— soaps, hair colorants, toiletries, and liquid detergents— flexibility serves as a major differentiator, giving it the ability to move much faster than multinational competitors. The flatness of its underlying structure allows the company to be lean and responsive so that it can respond quickly to changing market needs. It can make fast and flexible decisions when launching new products, while other firms react slowly to Godrej's maneuvers.

- Komsomolskaya Pravda might be among the oldest of Russia's leading publishers, but it's known more for its progressive management structure than for its long tenure. The company optimized its stakeholder structure from three hundred to thirty persons, leading to prompt decision making. With a collection of MBA programs and internships abroad for employees, a strong brand, and its general ability to develop managerial capabilities and retain those managers, it can provide a flexible corporate culture that is receptive to new business offers and feedback from employees. All of that allows it to better understand, as well as relate and react to, its reading audience.

Agility

Flexibility allows rough diamonds to adapt to changing market, institutional, and supply change conditions. Agility allows them to react faster and with more commitment than competitors can. We heard the word *flexibility* often in China, but it applies in all the BRIC countries. Firms have to be vigilant in seeking opportunities, because their fall could happen just as quickly and just as dramatically as the rise. An opportunity can morph into a legitimate threat if the company fails to respond quickly.

Chinese rough diamonds regard this potential volatility as an opportunity and have embedded agility as an innate characteristic of their company, a sort of gene that is part of their organizational systems. For example, moving quickly into a new market, as Linyang Group did with its smart electric meters and Beingmate did with its infant supplies, requires the type of quick and resolute decision making that comes only from a strong and innovative management structure built with agility in mind.

How agility manifests itself varies from company to company and country to country. Because Chinese rough diamonds tend to be relatively young and entrepreneurial, they had not yet developed the hierarchies or bureaucracies that were typical in state-owned enterprises, or in the more advanced, larger organizations, such as in Russia. But in many ways, the leadership in all the rough diamonds is similar to the visionary leaders in small, entrepreneurial upstarts in developed countries, such as those in California's Silicon Valley. Unencumbered by stockholders' pressures for short-term returns, the rough diamonds' CEOs are able to make decisions that might be unconventional and risky when viewed from a developed market.

Cohesiveness

Rough diamonds have built remarkably cohesive management structures, usually on the foundation of a resilient corporate culture. Madam Min Yang, the chair of Hanking Group, believes a corporate culture is the true soul of an enterprise. Companies have to create a culture that inspires the enthusiasm and realizes the potential of its employees, she said, encouraging its workers to make a concerted effort toward meeting the company's goals. Like so many other rough diamonds in China, the Hanking Group embedded a cohesive corporate culture by embracing the quintessential elements of traditional Chinese culture: it encourages employees to work hard and advocates a benevolence-oriented culture, which provides help for those who need it.

A similar example is Molong, a Chinese petroleum machinery firm. Enrong Zhang, the CEO of the company, created Molong's unique philosophy: "Stimulate the hearts, gather the minds, solidify the integrity, and create success for all." To instill these shared values throughout the company, Molong has built a recreation and sports center equipped with a library, chess room, gym, and other amenities in order to enrich workers' lives. The company has also established an internal competition system to encourage employees' creativity and enthusiasm, and it provides employees long-term career plans to retain talent. The mix of these practices attracts high-caliber professionals from China and overseas.

As we repeatedly found during our research, that sense of team and cohesiveness has become a key talent draw for many of the rough diamonds. Wellhope Agri-Tech, an animal feed–producing firm in China, has adopted an open owner-ship structure that passes down equity stakes to new layers of management over time. Initially the firm had only seven shareholders. In its fifth year, these seven cofounders awarded 25 percent of their shares to eighteen of the company's well-educated young staff, a move that inspired the young workers and helped bring the firm to the next level of development. After ten years, those twenty-five shareholders sold part of their shares to another twenty-four excellent managers at a symbolic price. Such moves motivated and attracted talented people, which become the source of the firm's competitive advantage. "Knowledge is power and unity is power," said company chair-man Weidong Jin. "Those who contribute get the share—more contribution, more share."

Of course, this focus on cohesive management and inspi-rational culture extends far beyond China. India's Marico invests heavily in building a culture of risk taking, idea gen-eration, and empowering people. It carefully structured the organization to remain open, informal, and participative, all the while encouraging experimentation. Meritocracy serves as the underlying theme, and the company's flat structure and cross-functional forums facilitate the firm's innovation and growth strategy.

Many of the rough diamonds in Brazil have built cohesiveness and resilience through the influence of family ownership. These companies started as family businesses and passed control rights down to at least one generation, but throughout the transitions, they have sustained an efficient transfer of management, knowledge, and responsibility. Family ownership ensures that the managers, who are usually the next generation, have the opportunity to learn how to manage the firm without the immediate pressure of increasing short-term company performance (box 5.5).

Box 5.5 Arezzo's Cohesive Culture

Arezzo, a family-owned women's footwear company in Brazil, was founded by brothers Anderson and Jefferson Birman in 1972. Since then the firm has remained tightly controlled by the Birman family. That any family member has to gain extensive experience in the firm before they can join the top management echelon is company policy. Its current vice chairman, Alexandre Birman, has eighteen years of experience in the company. This mechanism ensures that each family member has an opportunity to learn the business by participating in it, while allowing them the room to make mistakes early in their career as they get experience and build expertise. In the family's view, a strong corporate culture is directly associated with a strong brand, so they also make sure that every employee understands the brand concept and works to deliver what is promised to customers. This family management structure creates a culture that reduces monitoring costs and increases management efficiency.

One of India's most successful rough diamonds has instilled cohesiveness through a collective commitment to trust, transparency, and individual growth. Titan empowers its people to make decisions and take risks, a trust that fosters innovation and spurs open discussions about avenues for future growth. By channeling those efforts from across the company, leaders can identify new areas of expansion and focus resources and skills across the entire organization. All its new ventures, including Fastrack, Helios, GlodPlus, and Eye, were initiated internally by the operating team. "Empowering people to take business risks and make decisions is the pathway to growth," said Bhaskar Bhat, Titan's managing director. "At Titan, our culture is one of trust, transparency and commitment to individuals' growth aspirations. All our successful new ventures were initiated and enabled by our very own people. We believe that for Titan to grow successfully, it is imperative that employees learn and grow faster."

Titan's management structure generates the cohesion, agility, and flexibility that define a rough diamond. For these exemplary firms, this structure—when combined with a keen focus on value-chain optimization, collaborative innovation, and quality assurances—underpins the operational excellence companies need to sustain success over the long term.

Ultimately the rough diamonds' operational excellence is the kernel from which several critical competencies develop. And while few outside observers look past the lower labor costs in these emerging markets, these additional operational and cost advantages are crucial when many competitors can access the same labor pool. Without the cost advantages gained through a sharp eye on operations, late entrants in industrialization cannot compete with established industry stalwarts in their own countries and elsewhere.

Of course, rough diamonds share this ability to craft operational excellence with market leaders in developed countries. Yet we found the focus and effort directed to these factors especially strong among these firms. While rough diamonds vary in their management structures, all developed similar systems to emphasize logistical efficiency, innovation, quality, and cohesion—all of which helped solidify the demand-side advantages they carved by capitalizing on late development and creating new segments in their existing markets.

The next step is to expand beyond existing markets and branch into new products and geographies. That goes to the heart of the last of the Four Cs.

6

Cultivating Profitable Growth

Unfettered growth in both domestic and global markets can be risky; managed growth needs to attend to specific contingencies. As with any aspiring firm, there are different trajectories to grow and to internationalize, each with benefits and risks.

> —SKOLKOVO Business School–Ernst & Young Institute for Emerging Market Studies, *Rough Diamonds: The 4Cs Framework for Sustained High Performance*

Their mastery of marketing, operations, and management systems, however, departs in context and intent from firms in developed countries, or even from firms in their own countries that became successful when markets were first opened.

> —SKOLKOVO Business School–Ernst & Young Institute for Emerging Market Studies, *Rough Diamonds: The 4Cs Framework for Sustained High Performance*

Of the Four Cs, growth strategies are among the most complex because the rough diamonds in the different BRIC countries have such diverse histories, legacies, and contingencies. In examining the growth paths, we found that Chinese firms are the most aggressive in diversification, Brazilian rough diamonds tend to take a more gradual stance, Russian companies tend to be more domestically focused, and the Indian rough diamonds are more internationally oriented.

Even with marketing savvy and operational excellence, rough diamonds cannot create sustained advantages without leveraging their competencies into continuous, profitable growth. They are often latecomers in a fairly competitive domestic market that can accommodate only so much demand. In order to take full advantage of their scaled-up operations, rough diamonds have to explore new domestic profit sanctuaries, if not participate in the global market as a whole.

Because rough diamonds have grown faster than most other firms in the past decades, it is important for them to manage growth effectively. To succeed as they expand, these firms have to be able to both build on their local skills and competencies and push those skills into new territories. Unfettered growth in both domestic and global markets comes with risks, including what we call the "growth fetish" or a misplaced goal of companies to grow for the sake of growth but without due consideration of consequences. (We discuss this in chapter 7.) So companies must manage their expansion and diversification well to accommodate market-to-market differences and the ongoing internal challenges of growth.

We posed this question during our research: Is there an optimal method by which rough diamonds in emerging markets manage their sustained growth? This formed the basis for the last of the Four Cs: cultivating profitable growth. In comparing patterns of expansion and diversification with the historical experiences of firms in developed countries, we found that the rough diamonds are particularly attentive to both profitability and growth. This means they must attend to complex trade-offs between sales growth and profits, which we discuss in the next chapter.

Before we get to that point, we look at how companies first cultivate new growth opportunities. For rough diamonds, growth tends to stem primarily from a strategy of product diversification: entering new, related, or even unrelated businesses and markets in anticipation of the growth potential there. Such successful product diversification strategies not only increase the size of these firms; they also lead to improvements in operational efficiency by more effectively allocating resources across the entire value chain.

Our research revealed three primary factors that influence a firm's sustained performance: the direction, the speed and extent, and the mode of product diversification. Rough diamonds might put different weight on each variable for different decisions, but in one way or another, each of them factors into every product-diversification strategy.

THE DIRECTION OF ROUGH DIAMOND DIVERSIFICATION

The direction of a product diversification strategy often arises as the first question managers have to answer. These decisions typically break down into one of three categories: horizontal diversification, vertical integration, and diversification into unrelated fields (table 6.1). The direction of diversification is critical because this variable opens up a broad range of both risks and benefits. Moving into an unrelated field or market might test a company's core competencies, while expanding in a similar field can tax a firm's ability to scale its operations.

Like many other aspiring firms, rough diamonds must balance the benefits and risks of these moves. After all, the decision to diversify heavily into another business or country can set up a firm for long-term success or send it stumbling into a difficult recovery. It's not the right move for every company.

TABLE 6.1   Types of Product Diversification

	Related Diversification		Unrelated Diversification
	Horizontal Diversification	**Vertical Integration**	
Definition	Entering into a business that is closely related to a firm's current business	Entering into the business of a firm's upstream suppliers or downstream buyers	Entering into an unrelated business to a firm's current business
Rationales	Exploiting existing resources or capabilities into technology or customer-related markets	Ensuring stability of supply and demands Reducing transaction costs	Using slack resources Leaving current business to compete in markets with more potential Risk reduction
Example	A passenger car manufacturer moving into truck manufacturing	A dairy firm entering into the business of raising milk cows	A TV manufacturing firm entering the real estate business

While some rough diamonds have diversified widely and found great success, some of the others have reached their heights by diversifying within their existing fields (table 6.2).

In general, we found that the growth management of rough diamonds tends to differ by country. Overall, rough diamonds are actively involved in product diversification. More than 80 percent of these firms diversified into at least one other business, including at least 70 percent of the rough diamonds in each country. Slightly more than half of them diversified into horizontal, related businesses, and 57 percent

TABLE 6.2 Product Diversification and Internationalization of Rough Diamonds

	Total Diversi- fication	Related Diversification		Unrelated Diversi- fication	Export	Foreign Direct Invest- ment
		Horizontal Diversi- fication	Vertical Integra- tion			
China	100%	69%	69%	50%	94%	56%
Brazil	94	69	56	19	53	35
India	72	36	52	16	70	37
Russia	70	30	50	0	16	5
Total	81	51	57	22	59	34

diversified into vertically integrated businesses. Of the total, 22 percent diversified into unrelated businesses, with more than half of those in China.

Because horizontal-related diversification exploits a firm's existing assets and capabilities, it doesn't require a lot of new resources or capabilities. It's therefore generally considered the easiest and safest strategy among the three. This probably explains the high percentage of firms that have focused on related diversification. However, a closer examination of the data shows that only 42.6 percent diversified firms opted for related diversification as their first move. Instead, 46.3 percent of them chose a vertical integration strategy first, emphasizing the importance that many rough diamonds have put on strategy as a foundation for growth. In all four BRIC countries, more than half of the firms diversified first into vertically integrated businesses, and most of them did so early on.

The relatively underdeveloped market institutions in emerging markets make vertical integration an often necessary early step toward profitable growth. To overcome the lack of regulations that would ensure the sanctity of contracts with outside companies, many successful firms chose to internalize their transactions instead. This also gives a company more control over its inbound and outbound logistics, an especially important issue in countries that lack an established infrastructure. Not only does this allow companies to build scale and extend control across more of the value chain; it allows them to better manage their sales networks and collaborate better with distributors to make sure their products are delivered as promised.

THE SPEED AND EXTENT OF ROUGH DIAMOND DIVERSIFICATION

After discerning the direction in which to diversify, companies must ask how far and how fast. The speed and extent to which product diversification takes place has a critical impact on the long-term success of the strategy. Clearly some firms tend to be more aggressive than others (table 6.3). The Chinese rough diamonds diversify faster and further than firms in the other BRIC countries. Rough diamonds in Brazil diversify widely as well, but they tend to deliberate longer before jumping into their first diversification strategy.

TABLE 6.3   Speed and Extent of Product Diversification for Rough Diamonds

	China	Russia	India	Brazil	Average
Time length (years) between founding and the first diversification	9.13	21.5	15.41	36.73	20.15
Number of other business entered	3.38	0.90	1.6	2.38	2.10

EXAMINING THE MODE OF PRODUCT DIVERSIFICATION

With decisions about the direction, speed, and extent of the diversification strategy in place, companies must then figure out the best mode of diversification to reach those goals. Companies tend to follow three primary modes when they diversify into other businesses: greenfield, merger and acquisition (M&A), or joint venture (table 6.4).[1] A greenfield strategy channels investment into something that previously didn't exist, such as

TABLE 6.4 Modes of Product Diversification

	Greenfield	Merger and Acquisition	Joint Venture
Definition	Building a new plant	Merging with or acquiring an existing firm	Creating a new entity with another firm
Advantages	Complete control over the new plant No need to search for targets or partner No risk of technology or knowledge leakage	Faster access to markets The possibility of paying a low price for valuable assets	Pooling resources from two parties to achieve a larger scale Benefiting from complementary assets from a partner Risk reduction
Disadvantages	Slower to implement Requires a large amount of resources	Post M&A coordination Risk of selecting the wrong targets Risk of overpaying	Search for partners Risk of technology or knowledge leakage Conflicts with partners about how to manage the venture

an innovative new subsidiary or the construction of new factory, office, or R&D space. In essence, the firm creates a brand-new business from scratch using its own resources and efforts. M&A strategies are what you'd expect: the acquisition or combination of different companies or similar entities. A joint venture is a business agreement in which parties agree to develop, for a finite time, a new entity by contributing equity.

Each of the three modes of diversification has its own benefits and costs. An M&A approach, for example, often proves to be the fastest because a company acquires existing assets and doesn't have to build much, if anything, from scratch. Joint ventures tend to work best for businesses that require large upfront investment because it splits the high costs among multiple parties. Because the selection of diversification mode depends on a firm's own needs, no general rule governs the selection process. Managers need to carefully weigh the advantages and disadvantages of each entry mode. Choosing the wrong one can quickly jeopardize the entire diversification strategy.

Our research shows that rough diamonds prefer greenfield diversification as the primary mode of entry into a new business, regardless of the type of product diversification they pursue (figure 6.1). This tends to make sense given the low levels of trust and high transaction costs prevalent in emerging markets. Since M&A and joint venture strategies involve an outside party, rough diamonds can reduce their uncertainty by adopting a greenfield mode.

Rough diamonds are more likely to choose an M&A approach when they're pursuing unrelated diversification, which virtually always takes them into a business they're not familiar with. By acquiring or merging with a known, existing firm in that business, companies can often save the time and effort of developing the new expertise required in that field.

FIGURE 6.1 Types of Diversification and Entry Modes Adopted by the Rough Diamonds Percentage of RDs That Adopt This Specific Type of Entry Percentage

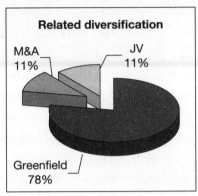

Related diversification

M&A 11%

JV 11%

Greenfield 78%

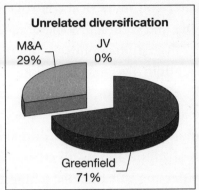

Unrelated diversification

M&A 29%

JV 0%

Greenfield 71%

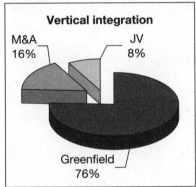

Vertical integration

M&A 16%

JV 8%

Greenfield 76%

In the case of vertical integration, companies are typically purchasing an existing supplier or buyer—a firm with which they have a higher degree of familiarity and trust.

Joint ventures are the least adopted entry mode among the three, due mainly to the difficulty in selecting an appropriate partner for investing with. Our research found that six of the eleven rough diamonds that entered into joint ventures did so with foreign partners. In these cases, the foreign partner was generally well known, had an established reputation, and owned advanced technologies. For example, Lakshmi Machine Works, an Indian textile machinery manufacturer, started to produce computer numerical control machine tools through a partnership and technical collaboration with Mori Seiki of Japan.

Rough diamonds in different countries displayed different trends in diversification modes (table 6.5). Compared with their Russian, Indian, and Brazilian counterparts, Chinese rough diamonds tend to be more active in establishing joint ventures when pursuing related diversification and vertical integration strategies. Most of them partnered with foreign companies, reflecting the broader Chinese intention to access advanced technologies and bring them to the domestic marketplace.

TABLE 6.5   Entry Modes of Product Diversification for Rough Diamonds

		Related Diversification	Unrelated Diversification	Vertical Integration
Greenfield	Overall	78.18%	70.83%	76.56%
	China	68.42	78.57	76.19
	Russia	66.67	0	66.67
	India	93.33	60.00	85.00
	Brazil	77.78	60.00	70.59
M&A	Overall	10.91	29.17	15.63
	China	5.26	21.43	14.29
	Russia	33.33	0	0
	India	0	40.00	10.00
	Brazil	22.22	40.00	29.41
JV	Overall	10.91	0	7.81
	China	26.32	0	9.52
	Russia	0	0	33.33
	India	6.67	0	5.00
	Brazil	0	0	0

Although Chinese firms take this aggressive approach to product diversification, they rarely select the fastest mode of entry: M&A. We attribute this to several factors. First, the lack of trust and information forces Chinese rough diamonds to take a more cautious approach to outside firms. Second, they lack appropriate, available, and suitable targets. Many of the available targets are bankrupt state-owned enterprises, and most Chinese business leaders believe that private firms will have difficulty integrating a formerly state-owned business. And third, given the abundant labor and other raw materials in China, greenfield investments can get up to speed faster than in many other countries.

Brazilian rough diamonds tend to adopt an M&A approach more than their counterparts from other countries. Because Brazil has a longer market-based history than other countries, the domestic market is mature and saturated, making many existing firms credible candidates for merger or acquisition.

Despite the fact that Russia, like China, experienced remarkable economic liberalization during the 1990s, Russian companies did not enjoy the same abundant opportunities that Chinese companies had. During the posttransition period from planned economy during 1980s and 1990s in China, privatization led to intense market competition in most sectors. The same level of competition did not occur in Russia, which also suffered from weaker market institutions and a lower level of trust. Because of those factors, the Russian rough diamonds immediately focused on enhancing and solidifying their market positions in their existing markets and areas. Not surprisingly, none of the Russian firms on our list diversified into unrelated businesses.

DIFFERENT COUNTRIES SPAWN DIFFERENT GROWTH PATTERNS

The external environment has a major influence on how companies select the direction, speed, extent, and mode of their diversification strategies. Different BRIC countries spawn distinctive growth paths and competencies. To be sure, rough diamonds excel at management through transitions no matter the external environment (box 6.1). But part of their success stems from their ability to understand the business environment around them and adopt strategies that account for the environment in which they're operating.

China's Rough Diamonds: Exploiting Rapid and Broad Diversification

Chinese firms are the most actively diversified in terms of both products and geography. Because many industries in China were not well developed in earlier years, they were not saturated with competitors. As long as these firms can enter these industries, they can become first movers and benefit from such advantages. But not all firms have the capacity to enter these markets efficiently. Companies might see these open opportunities and move quickly to capitalize on them, but sustained success requires the right skills and resources. Still, with so many underserved, potentially huge markets in China, most of the rough diamonds in our study would have the requisite skills to diversify successfully into both related and unrelated businesses quickly.

Chinese rough diamonds also tend to participate in international expansion at earlier stages of development. Participating in global competition not only provides them with an important avenue through which to achieve sustainable growth; it also equips them with invaluable knowledge on how to adapt to local environments and operate successfully in foreign

Box 6.1 Growth Patterns: What Is Different About Emerging Markets?

In a landmark study published in 1962, *Strategy and Structure*, economic historian Alfred P. Chandler studied the growth and evolution of America's seventy largest enterprises. Among his conclusions, which spurred a flurry of follow-up research and similar studies across several continents, Chandler argued that these firms followed a staged progression of growth that's based on their efficiency. Firms adopted strategies and structures that reflected incremental changes, from expansion, to vertical integration, to related and unrelated diversification.

Chandler's conclusions prompted later scholars, notably Jay Galbraith and Daniel Nathanson, to formulate a congruence hypothesis, in which the performance of a firm would depend on the extent to which its structures and efficiencies were aligned with its strategies. In our study of rough diamonds, we confirmed a similar pattern of gradual diversification (although Chinese firms were more aggressive than their peers in other BRIC countries). Even so, some nuanced differences reflect the evolving institutional landscape of emerging markets:

- *A concern for profitability in addition to growth*. Clearly growth considerations manifest themselves in product diversification, but growth in and of itself is not the determining factor. The drive for high profits is. (We discuss this further in chapter 8.)

- *Cultural and institutional influences*. The Brazilian rough diamonds paid a lot of attention to brand legacies. Chinese firms relied more on their relationships, Indian companies tended to focus on their longer history of international trade, and Russian companies capitalized on domestic opportunities that arose from geographical advantages.

- *Limitations of economic and institutional environment*. Rough diamonds in emerging markets pursue fewer mergers and acquisitions, in part because those economies lack viable candidates, but also because of the inherent limitations of capital and equity markets in those countries.

Sources: Alfred P. Chandler, *Strategy and Structure* (Cambridge, MA: MIT Press, 1962); Jay Galbraith and Daniel Nathanson, *Strategy Implementation: The Role of Structure and Process* (St. Paul, MN: West, 1978).

countries. Most of these firms started exporting their products within the first decade after their founding, primarily due to the low cost of expansion and their increasing technological competence (box 6.2).

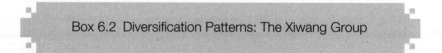

Box 6.2 Diversification Patterns: The Xiwang Group

The Xiwang Group, a Chinese leader in starch and starch-related products, is a good example of broad diversification. Located in Xiwang Village in Shandong Province in northeast of China, it started from the corn processing industry and gradually diversified into related and unrelated businesses. It purchased a technology that processed sugar from cornstarch into glycerol, a soapy sweet fluid. Following a market slump, it also found ways to process that glycerol into the production of glutamate, a type of salt from glutamic acid. Vertically, it expanded further into logistics and heat power. Horizontally, it expanded again, moving into industries such as beverages and biochemical products. And it moved into unrelated industries, including real estate, steel, and investment. All the while, it began its move outside the Chinese market by exporting to Asia, Europe, and the Middle East. The company eventually started its own import and export trading company, with subsidiaries in Hong Kong and South Korea.

Chinese firms also display a unique ability to leverage their relationships when developing and implementing their marketing and operational strategies. Because relationships are not bounded by industry, Chinese rough diamonds relentlessly use those connections to support their push into unrelated diversification paths. We found that the level to which CEOs rise in the People's Congress, or China's highest legislative body, can serve as a close proxy for the depth and breadth of their relationships. Generally the higher the rise in the People's Congress, the more connected the person is. CEOs who are elected as deputies to the People's Congress are widely seen as especially well-connected businesspeople whose firms could be better suited for diversification strategies (tables 6.6 and 6.7).

As tables 6.6 and 6.7 show, firms that undertake unrelated diversification and vertical integration strategies typically have CEOs who serve as deputies to the national or provincial levels of the People's Congress. Similar patterns can be found in vertical integration. The firms led by these higher-level, connected CEOs take less time before moving into their first diversification, and they tend to enter more different businesses. Although certainly this is not a causal association, this preliminary analysis

TABLE 6.6 CEOs as Deputies in the People's Congress, by Type of Diversification

	National	Provincial	City	District	Village	Not Served
Number of firms	4	4	5	1	0	2
Unrelated diversified	3	3	1	1	0	0
Vertically integrated	4	4	2	0	0	1

TABLE 6.7 Number of CEOs as Deputies in the People's Congress, by Diversification Time and Other Businesses Entered

	National	Provincial	City	District	Village	Not Served
Number of firms	4	4	5	1	0	2
Time (years) between founding and the first diversification	5.25	6.5	9.2	14	0	9
Number of other business entered	5.25	3.5	2.2	2	0	3

suggests a fairly strong correlation between greater relational capital and more aggressive diversification patterns.[2]

Brazilian Rough Diamonds: Attention to Gradual Diversification

Brazil's rough diamonds rank second in terms of diversification. Because most of these firms have long histories and strong brand legacies, they can better establish their advantage in new markets, including in other countries. Thus, a high percentage of Brazilian firms invest in unrelated businesses. Although these firms diversify extensively, they do not rush into these strategies as quickly as their counterparts in China do. Instead, they adopt a gradual diversification strategy that usually starts with related diversification before moving into unrelated businesses. This incremental approach mitigates the risks that come with rapid expansion and allows them to deliberately build on their already established legacies.

Screw manufacturer Ciser exemplifies this gradual approach to diversification. In the years after its 1959 launch, Ciser's product portfolio consisted of furniture, electronic hardware, and civil construction. In 1967, it extended its business to screws and nuts for civil construction, railroads, and metal mechanics. In the 1970s, it expanded its product range further. And in 1978, it opened a sales office and a distribution center in São Paulo, which gave it a strong market position for standardized screws and nuts in Brazil.

Only then did the company start to seriously consider other expansion possibilities. Since 1980, it has been aggressively pursuing the transportation business sector, which has the added advantage of providing transportation for a wide range of its products and components. And after vertically integrating its entire value chain, the firm put the lessons it learned to work in new territories. In 1981, it acquired 166 hectares of land in

Araquari, in the northern region of Santa Catarina, to breed wild boars, buffalo, and cattle. In 1984, the company managed and sold land, houses, apartments, and areas for commercial, industrial, and agricultural use. It started exporting in 1972 and now sells products in more than twenty countries around the world, including China, the United States, Japan, and Canada. The company's sustained growth reflects the critical balance it has struck between adequate control (vertical integration) and market opportunities (unrelated businesses).

Russian Rough Diamonds: Focused on Domestic Growth

Russian companies did not enjoy the same abundant opportunities that opened up in China during the posttransition period, when privatization led to intense market competition in most industry sectors. Moreover, the weak institutions and the generally low level of trust in Russian society hindered the growth and success of many entrepreneurial Russian firms. The combination forced most firms to focus locally, so they could capture, solidify, and enhance their positions in their own markets and industries. As a result, none of the Russian rough diamonds conducted diversification in unrelated businesses, and even now, only a few of them have exported or pursued foreign direct investment.

Most of the Russian rough diamonds were born, or reborn, as private firms in the mid- to late 1990s, when their markets were competitive, fragmented, and embryonic. Their first phase of growth centered on building competitiveness in the domestic market, mostly through strategies to increase operational scale, achieve cost advantages, or establish brand saturation across different market segments that would allow them to establish pricing advantages. One example is NEP LL, the market leader in tea and coffee production, which scaled up and gained cost and price advantages over its competitors. Its separation from the rest of the pack began between 1999 and 2001, when Leningrad's regional government helped the company expand its tea production volume from 14,400 tons to 30,000 tons, all while doubling its coffee capacity as well.

Velkom, the producer of several hundred different food products, pursued a complex, within-product diversification that adjusted brands and prices for a wide range of quality and income levels within each product category. In this process, the company learned what worked and what didn't at each phase of its expansion. Other rough diamonds increased their visibility and competitiveness by tapping into the resources of a larger conglomerate. These large group companies offer instant access to the logistical services, market intelligence, management skills, and capital possessed by the group as a whole, a coveted asset when pursuing broad cost or differentiation strategies (box 6.3).

Russia's rough diamonds pursued regional and product diversification only after securing their competitive advantage in established market niches. Again, unlike the Chinese entrepreneurs that aggressively moved into unrelated areas for new applications and better opportunities, these Russian firms continued to stay within their own familiar areas of expertise when expanding into new markets and regions. For example, Mordovtsement engaged in a focused geographical expansion even as market competition intensified. Throughout the frenzy of privatization, it expanded at a measured pace, opening thirty-one new regional subsidiaries since 1992 in order to stay closer to its core customers.

In short, while Chinese and Brazilian rough diamonds pursued aggressive globalization and diversification into unrelated product areas, their counterparts in Russia remained more conservative and focused on local markets and product categories. In our view, weak formal institutions and lack of

Box 6.3 MLVZ's Approach to Diversification-Leveraged Management Systems

Alfred Chandler argued in his authoritative study of organizational structure that companies had to design their business in a manner that supports the requirements of its growth strategy. This, of course, is much easier said than done, but MLVZ's decisions reflected the deliberate and purposeful choices that Chandler outlined. "Besides our own unique strengths, we obtained strong brands, powerful support of the company's central apparatus and unique opportunities of intra-corporate interaction with other members of the Synergiya Group," said Prokhorov Konstantin Anatolevich, the firm's general director. "It is obvious that all mentioned instruments of related diversification are realized in the complex holding structure of 'Synergiya' company. In such a way, using related diversification, we remain in our market segment and try to strengthen in it."

Although the internationalization strategies adopted by Russia's rough diamonds were limited in terms of geographical coverage and the extent of their operations, several of them did venture into other Commonwealth of Independent States countries. But most of them, including MLVZ, took gradual steps down this path. MLVZ limited itself to exporting for a while, but with that in place, it moved beyond its comfort zone to pursue what became a richly successful cross-marketing alliance with an international firm, William Grant & Sons, one of the top scotch whisky producers. "We have achieved internationalization as Beluga is sold all over the world," Prokhorov said. "A significant step to internationalization was forming the alliance with a world leader in the alcohol business, William Grant & Sons. While we cross-market each other's products, we were able to enhance the portfolio of our brands domestically. Whisky is a growing sector in Russia, and it does not compete with vodka. In a word, in everything we do, we try to achieve a synergistic effect to justify and strengthen our brand."

trust explain the higher dependence on this greenfield strategy. Even so, this gradual process of internationalization should not be interpreted as exhibiting weak management. The record established by these Russian rough diamonds obviously proves otherwise. Their disciplined management approach merely focuses on related-diversification strategies, reflecting their quest for synergy and organic growth instead of risky international business opportunities.

Indian Rough Diamonds: Focused Diversification and Internationalization

Much like their Russian counterparts, Indian rough diamonds followed carefully managed diversification plans. Instead of pursuing broad diversification, they chose to remain focused and sought growth by enhancing and solidifying the market positions they had built in their domestic markets. Nevertheless, Indian rough diamonds clearly are more active in some internationalization activities, such as exporting. Moreover, they have maintained a strategy to explore foreign markets with their low-cost products (box 6.4).

Box 6.4 Bombay Rayon Fashion: Gradual But Focused International Growth

Bombay Rayon Fashions, established by Janardhan Agrawal in 1986, started by manufacturing woven fabric in Maharashtra. In 1998, the firm opened another manufacturing facility for woven fabric and began to export its products. In 2001, it became vertically integrated by starting a garment business and in 2003 started exporting garment products. Two years later, it was publicly listed on all the stock exchanges in India.

Bombay Rayon Fashions eventually expanded its manufacturing capacity with seven garment manufacturing facilities in Bangalore that housed seventy thousand machines. It also acquired U.K.-based DPJ Clothing and started supplying garments to high-end retailers in the United Kingdom. In 2007, it acquired Leela Scottish Lace, one of the largest garment-manufacturing firms in India, and LNJ Apparel, making it one of the largest apparel firms in India. The firm added the iconic brand Guru the following year.

Most of India's rough diamonds follow a narrow growth path. They do not expand heavily into other businesses, preferring to stay focused on their primary product markets. They increase capacity and reach market leadership by setting up new facilities or acquiring existing plants. However, their internationalization activities tend to start relatively early in their development. But even here, they take a fairly deliberate approach. They begin by exporting their products, due to the low cost advantage, and only after gaining exporting experience do they begin more radical internationalization through foreign direct investment. They eventually become true global players by acquiring foreign firms.

Perhaps as much in India as in any of the other BRIC countries, the nature of technology also helps determine the path of diversification, whether in related or unrelated businesses. For example, Tata Metaliks pioneered the production of high-quality pig iron, a niche market product at the time. Since then it has moved into a related business, ductile iron pipes, and gradually expanded its presence in foreign markets. Tata Metaliks made a conscious effort not to enter any unrelated businesses or engage in vertical integration that could damage its technological advantage.

What's clear is that Tata Metaliks and the other rough diamonds in all the BRIC countries capitalized on diversification plans that suited both their internal operations and the markets they pursued. While firms in different countries adopted different approaches, all of them capitalized on the advantages afforded them without being burdened by unnecessary risk. Their success at leveraging advantage is reflected in market positions around the world.

When looking across all the Four Cs for sustaining high performance, we can see that the rough diamonds took a similar overarching strategy and adapted it to pave their various paths to success. However, their mastery of marketing, operations, and management systems differs from firms in developed countries and even from many of the large, incumbent firms in their own countries. Admittedly, a number of external factors, such as changed governmental regulations and market liberalization, arrived with serendipitous timing. But rough diamonds took advantage of and capitalized on those opportunities, and they have sustained that success.

7

How Rough Diamonds Avoid the Growth Fetish

Growth is clearly desirable, if not a mandate in emerging markets, but what type of growth? An overemphasis on firm growth can lead to a "growth fetish," where growth is unqualified and seen as an end in itself. This type of growth can easily lead to overextension and is particularly acute in emerging markets because manufacturing facilities, managerial talents, and physical infrastructure—all requisites that support growth—are limited by underdeveloped market institutions.

—SKOLKOVO Business School–Ernst & Young Institute for Emerging Market Studies, *Rough Diamonds: The 4Cs Framework for Sustained High Performance*

By 2012, the increased visibility of emerging markets and their role in the global economic recession prompted a key question: Can emerging markets sustain their high growth? Examining a broad sample of 105,260 BRIC companies, we find that firms with an initial focus on profits are better able to combine sustained high profits and high revenue. Using a subset of rough diamonds, we find they accomplish this dual growth through qualified expansion and by nurturing their core competencies.

The 2007–2009 Great Recession kindled two widely held beliefs among business pundits. First, the conventional wisdom held that worldwide growth would remove the shackles of the economic stagnation. Second, while growth in all quarters of the world is desirable, the primary source of economic expansion will come from emerging markets, where growth is expected to outpace the developed world by close to 3.5 percent.[1] Despite those assumptions, a persistent question remains about the pace of growth rates in these emerging economies.[2]

The same pundits who reached a broad consensus on the first two issues remain very much divided on the third. Optimists see sustained growth as more stable macroeconomic policies and conditions start to unleash the pent-up demand of a growing middle class. More skeptical observers believe the deceleration brought about by continuing stagnation in more developed countries, which fuel the emerging markets' exports, will continue to dampen economies worldwide.[3]

Sustainable growth depends largely on a rising gross domestic product (GDP) at the country level or the presence of high-performing firms at the industrial level. Historically, GDP has served as the primary indicator of growth. This gross measure can mislead, however, because it does not fully capture or distinguish certain critical factors of development, including improvements in education, legal statutes, governance structures, and infrastructures. These factors clearly undergird emerging and developing economies, yet they often are not reflected in top-line GDP calculations.

Moreover, the high-level economic indicators often obscure or overlook the distinctive contributions of both incumbent market leaders and rapidly developing companies. Granted, focusing on market leaders and growth firms, the favored method of prior studies to assess national prominence, can produce skewed results. Companies' performances depend on the type of growth strategy they adopt and the measure used to appraise it. So instead, we've focused on the rough diamonds' growth strategies and how those approaches lead to sustained growth over time.

Clearly companies want to grow. Indeed, they have to grow. But what type of growth should they pursue? Many companies in all kinds of markets have overemphasized growth for growth's sake—an unqualified and unbalanced approach to expansion that we call the growth fetish. But our research on more than 105,000 firms in the BRIC countries shows that the growth fetish is especially acute in emerging markets. Because underdeveloped market institutions often limit the capacity of manufacturing facilities, managerial talents, and physical infrastructure, all requisites for growth, many companies focus too narrowly on revenue and market share growth, with less regard for profitability.[4]

Rough diamonds, however, followed phased-in growth strategies that featured gradual and incremental expansion. And rather than expand just to get bigger, they focused on sustaining high levels of profitability. In this chapter, we advance a case for profitable growth: the integration of revenue and profits as the means to sustained success. The rough diamonds' long-term performance offers strong proof, but we've included a broader sample of BRIC companies here as a contrast to that sustained profitable growth at these exemplary firms.

WHAT IS SUSTAINABLE GROWTH?

With the pundits wondering whether emerging markets can sustain their growth, we asked a different set of questions: How do growth strategies at the firm level affect overall sustainability at the country level? And what can these exemplary firms teach us about sustainable growth?

More recent examinations of sustained growth generally define it as a qualified expansion that does not compromise the ecological or economic integrity of future generations.[5] After exploring the trade-offs between revenue growth and profit maximization, we boiled our definition down to the idea of profitable growth: a concurrent focus on both high profits and high sales that underpins a firm's sustained success. Without sales, a firm has no profits, and without profits, a firm cannot reinvest in its operations to expand its revenue. This all sounds straightforward enough, but it is an especially critical point for companies in emerging economies, where access to capital markets is restricted or cut off entirely. Unlike their counterparts in developed countries, which enjoy the relative luxury of accessible debt and equity markets, companies in emerging countries must rely much more heavily, and sometimes entirely, on their own resources. (More broadly, we would argue that growth in emerging markets also very much depends on internal resources and the collection of domestic companies that sustain a high level of performance over the long term.)

To develop a more empirical understanding of why profitable growth is so important to these companies, industries, and countries, we developed a far-reaching sample by compiling company-level data across multiple key sectors in the BRIC countries. The sample data were compiled from 2002 to 2011 on more than 105,000 firms. By parsing through the data, we identified the initial decisions these firms made regarding their growth strategies. Did they focus more on sales or profits, and which path led to sustained development over time?

We considered two five-year phases: 2002–2006 and 2007–2011. In each phase, we broke down the field of companies into four categories using our own detailed studies and a baseline of average industry sales and profit growth data for the time period in question:

- High sales growth/high profit growth (HH)
- High sales growth/low profit growth (HL)
- Low sales growth/high profit growth (LH)
- Low sales growth/low profit growth (LL)

Most of the previous studies we reviewed based their results primarily on data from listed firms. But because most emerging-market companies are not publicly listed, we amassed data from thousands of unlisted firms to provide a more comprehensive picture of growth management in the BRIC countries.

Ultimately sustainable growth refers not just to enduring performance but also to a consistently positive total growth trajectory. This more holistic approach allows us to weed out the companies that put up remarkable numbers in one category or over one five-year period from the ones that show sustained strength across the full set of measures and time periods. This is how we define profitable growth.

SALES OR PROFITS? AN OVERVIEW OF BRIC COMPANIES

After combing through reams of data, information from secondary sources, and extensive interviews with company leaders, we found that managers make certain initial decisions about how they will expand. Their strategy is either sales oriented or profit oriented.[6] Typically each strategy comes with its own set of trade-offs. A sales-oriented company might initially sacrifice profits in order to carve out a larger market share, hoping to ignite profit growth later. This approach is especially common in maturing markets, where companies are scrambling to stake their claim and establish their brand. A profit-oriented firm will limit expenses in order to maintain a desired level of net income; by doing so, though, it might miss out on limited opportunities to expand markets and market share (table 7.1).

Admittedly, the trade-off between profits and sales is a well-trod path in the business-growth literature. However, this research differs on several fronts. First, it shifts that focus on a huge database of firms in developed countries to emerging economies.[7] These companies and the environment in which they operate sharply differ from companies in developed

TABLE 7.1   Key Differences Between Profit- and Sales-Oriented Companies

Description	Profit Oriented	Sales Oriented
Objective	Demonstrate a steady and reliable flow of profits for external and internal operations	Harness a formidable market position by attaining a targeted market share
Focus	Return on sales; cost efficiency; emphasis on operational activities	Market share; sales growth; unit cost economies; can include acquisitions that broaden market scope
Key performance criteria	Return on invested capital	Market share; relative market share
Requirements for success	Cost control; high profit margins to cover operational and nonoperational expenses	Scale and scope economies; effective marketing corresponding to segment needs
Favored growth trajectory	Related diversification; vertical integration	Related and unrelated diversification; acquisitions

countries, where, for example, capital markets and established institutions are readily available. Second, we found three primary characteristics that distinguished emerging markets from developed ones:

- *Fast growth in a relatively short time.* The rapid pace of growth in emerging markets, a benefit, nevertheless can present a host of challenges. Growth requires successive investments, and firms have to concurrently build capital and other investment resources while retaining their strategic focus.

- *The lack of supportive macroeconomic and institutional factors.* The comparatively underdeveloped institutions in emerging markets create higher transactional costs. This puts a higher premium on informal institutions such as norms, values, culture, and relationship networks. As institutions develop, companies have to balance their strategies and tactics with the rising influence of formal market exchanges, informational certainty, technological innovations, and formal legal statutes.[8] How to achieve sustainable profitable growth within a transitional environment is an especially critical factor for success in emerging markets.

- *Unique company resources and capabilities.* In part because of the less developed institutions, companies in these markets rely more on their own resources and abilities. Firms in developed countries can typically rely on innovation and marketing capabilities. For companies that face changing environments, different sets of capabilities, such as a rich network of relationships, take priority. Sustained, profitable growth depends on a company's ability to tap into these alternative resources and capabilities.

With the unique backdrop of emerging markets in place, we can revisit some of the key questions about profitable growth. With limited resources, which path should firms take toward growth? Given their unique market conditions, should they sacrifice sales growth for profitability, or vice versa? The answers to these questions are not evident, of course, but the experiences of the more than 105,000 companies we studied offer some valuable lesson. We can learn from successful firms how they use a variety of strategies to achieve profitable growth. We then can take a closer look at the strategies these rough diamonds employed.

NOT ALL GROWTH IS GOOD

Overall GDP growth provides firms in emerging markets the opportunity to expand rapidly, but fast growth doesn't always translate to sustained growth. Unlike large multinationals based in developed countries, firms in emerging markets, especially those in China and Russia, typically have less experience operating in a market-based economy. Growth in these countries often increases hand-in-hand with the release of pent-up market demand, the emergence of new consumers, and the evolution of new market segments. As so often happens in developed economies, greater size is equated to greater market power.[9]

Profit Impact of Market Strategy (PIMS) studies say that market share is inextricably tied to profitability. High market share might initially lead to lower profits, but as companies increase their scale and scope, the resulting economies lead to lower per unit costs and, by extension, greater profitability.[10] The PIMS studies indicate that market leaders enjoy a range of tangible and intangible benefits of market power, including lower advertising costs, lower variable costs, lower research costs, and even lower labor costs.

In emerging markets, however, sustained growth does not stem from an unqualified pursuit of more sales and assets to gain market dominance. Rather, the growth management strategies become increasingly important as companies in these markets expand. Increased size, for example, often leads to greater need for coordination and more careful management across the value chain.[11] Responsibly managed rough diamonds do not always get the headlines that hypergrowth companies might attract, but they consistently return better results over time.

The lack of control is exacerbated in emerging markets, where a lack of professional managers and talent persists. Excessive growth in a relatively short time can create dysfunction if a company doesn't concurrently build the corresponding resources and capabilities, such as manufacturing facilities and managerial competencies. Moreover, unless these firms achieve economies of scale as they expand, expenses will exceed revenues and eat into profits.

Ultimately the key to achieving sustainable growth is not growth itself but profitable growth over time. In our study, the firms that overemphasized growth at the expense of profitability were eventually blindsided by management control problems or surpassed by smaller, more nimble competitors.

EXAMINING GROWTH TRAJECTORIES IN THE BRICS: FOUR SCENARIOS

To better understand how vital profitable growth is to companies in emerging markets, we classified all the firms we studied by growth and profitability and by time period. This presents

TABLE 7.2   Four Scenarios of Growth and Profitability

	High Profitability	**Low Profitability**
High sales growth	I. Profitable growth: the ideal state	II. Firms on the margin: unprofitable market leaders
Low sales growth	III. Firms in waiting: low growth but high profitability	IV. Declining firms: vacuous growth

four different growth trajectories (table 7.2).[12] Those that balance their rapid growth with strong profitability, for example, reach an ideal state for sustained success.

Not every firm can reach such a favorable position, which is why we call it an ideal state. The relationship between sales growth and profit in cell I is a complex one contingent on many internal and external factors: the stage of industry evolution, a prescient strategic analysis, and flawless execution, to name just a few. By contrast, firms with both low profitability and low sales growth, cell IV, have clearly entered into a period of decline—in many cases, a position from which struggling companies do not recover.

The intermediate states—what we call firms on the margin (cell II) and firms in waiting (cell III)—are the most interesting cases. These companies are intriguing because any future strategic choices on their part will spell the difference between sustained success and a spiral into contraction or obscurity. Although growing companies need to boost both sales and profitability, firms inevitably have to balance and prioritize them as market conditions and internal resources dictate.

A company that sees an opportunity to gain market share might move from the ideal state to become a firm on the margin, essentially sacrificing some profit to increase sales. That same company might later convert into a firm-in-waiting state, opting to scale back sales growth as it solidifies its internal operations to match the requirements of its market share gains. While companies might not consciously choose a sales-oriented or profit-oriented strategy, that preference inevitably manifests itself through the strategies they do choose deliberately.

To be sure, both sales-oriented and profit-oriented strategies can produce profitable growth. There is no preordained path. If a firm successfully executes a sales-oriented strategy early on, it can glean a profit later as it flexes the market muscle it gained. Strong market share usually results in greater economies of scale, as the PIMS studies attest. A profit-oriented strategy also can lead to greater sales growth and market leadership. High profit typically results from cost efficiency, cost reduction, a disciplined management culture, and a focus on standardized products. The ability to deploy these resources and capabilities in new businesses through thoughtful expansion strategies can deliver significant new market growth. Although these cases aren't as common, we discuss a few in this chapter.

Sales- and profit-oriented strategies can lead to profitable growth over time, but they require different resources and capabilities. The ability to develop the proper competencies distinguishes the level of firm performance and often influences strategy. Early decisions about how to grow—through sales or profits—usually relied on a company's intent and circumstances. But one thing was clear from our research: the different approaches led to different results (table 7.3).

Almost 37 percent of the companies that balanced high sales and profit growth in the first five-year phase were able to maintain that balance over time, and another 31 percent generated high profit even as sales growth decelerated. What we found for companies with high sales growth or high profit, but not both, was especially interesting. Of the initially sales-oriented firms, only 9.5 percent achieved profitability during

TABLE 7.3   Growth Trajectories

Phase I Status	Phase II HH	Phase II HL	Phase II LH	Phase II LL
High sales/high profit (profitable growth), HH	36.7%	16.9%	31.1%	15.3%
High sales/low profit (sales-oriented strategy), HL	9.5	40.5	8.4	41.6
Low sales/high profit (profit-oriented strategy), LH	35.3	13.2	36.2	15.3
Low sales/low profit, LL	11.5	34.3	10.8	43.5

Note: Phase I status covered 2006 to 2011; phase II covered 2007 to 2011.

the second five-year phase. And more than a third of the companies that initially focused on profit added strong sales growth over time. In the end, our research shows that a strategy focused initially on profit produced better results than one focused primarily on growth.

Taking a closer look at the data on firms that initially focused on one strategy or the other (see figures 7.1 to 7.5), we discovered some notable patterns in the movement of firms from the first five-year phase to the next. Firms that adopted a sales-oriented strategy in phase I are more likely to fall into the low growth/low profitability category in phase II. More than 70 percent of the firms that adopted a profit-oriented strategy in phase I retained their higher profitability in phase II. In other words, not only did an initial profit orientation tend to produce better results later, companies could more easily move from profit to sales than the opposite. Fewer than one in ten firms successfully made the switch from a sales-first strategy to a profit later.

FIGURE 7.1 Phase II Distribution of Growth-Oriented and Profit-Oriented Firms in Phase I

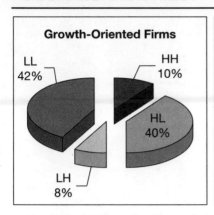
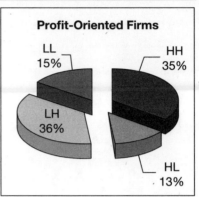

FIGURE 7.2 China: Phase II Distribution of Growth-Oriented and Profit-Oriented Firms in Phase I

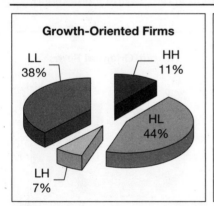
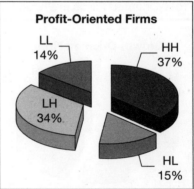

Note: N = 12,349 growth-oriented firms and 11,795 profit-oriented firms.

Firms that adopt a profit-oriented strategy in phase I are in a much better position to attain high sales growth later, and firms that initially adopt a sales growth strategy are less likely to reach high profitability over time. This finding is not consistent

FIGURE 7.3   Russia: Phase II Distribution of Growth-Oriented and Profit-Oriented Firms in Phase I

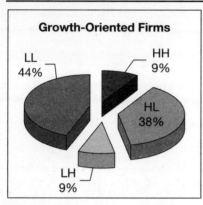
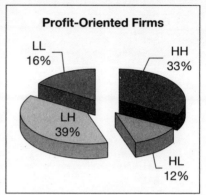

Note: N = 17,643 growth-oriented firms and 9,560 profit-oriented firms.

FIGURE 7.4   India: Phase II Distribution of Growth-Oriented and Profit-Oriented Firms in Phase I

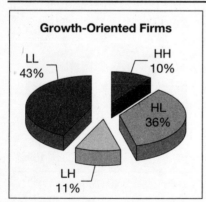
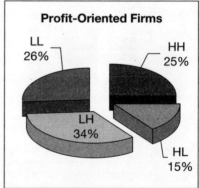

Note: N = 1,053 growth-oriented firms and 976 profit-oriented firms.

with some of the fundamental assertions of the PIMS reports, which suggest that high market share will ultimately lead to high profitability.

FIGURE 7.5   Brazil: Phase II Distribution of Growth-Oriented and Profit-Oriented Firms in Phase I

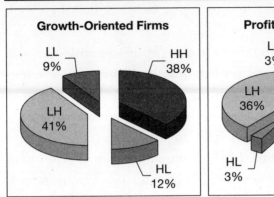
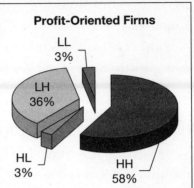

Note: N = 34 growth-oriented firms and 230 profit-oriented firms.

CROSS-COUNTRY DIFFERENCES

We discovered some varied trends when filtering the data nationally, but this overall trend held across the four BRIC countries. Chinese firms tended to jump out early and showed the highest probability of achieving both high sales growth and high profit during the first five-year phase. They tended to sustain that as well: they displayed a lower proclivity toward dropping into the tier of low profit and sales growth in the second five years. Generally the fast economic growth and stable policy environment in China provide its firms better opportunities to achieve profitable growth than firms in Russia and India (figure 7.2).

As would be expected given our overall findings, Russian firms tended to benefit most from a profit-oriented growth strategy (figure 7.3). A majority of firms that were initially oriented to sales growth kept their position as high sales growth, but only 9 percent moved into profitable growth. By contrast, a third of the companies that started out as profit oriented moved into high sales and high profit growth in the second five years—and almost four in ten at least retained their high profitability.

Fewer Indian firms moved from a profit orientation to high sales growth/high profit (only a quarter of them did so), and the possibility of dropping down into the bottom, low-growth tier was higher than other countries, at 26 percent (figure 7.4). This suggests that profit is hard to sustain in India, perhaps partly because it is home to fewer state-owned enterprises than in China and Russia. State-owned firms usually enjoy monopoly positions in profitable industries, whereas Indian companies face stiffer competition to sustain their profits and sales growth over time.

Brazil was the one exception to the patterns generally displayed across the other three BRIC countries (figure 7.5). This was due in large part to the small number of initially sales-oriented companies there, a likely result of the longer tenure of most Brazilian companies. We found only 34 Brazilian companies that focused on sales growth in the first five-year phase compared with 230 profit-oriented firms. Even so, the general pattern still holds: profit-oriented firms in phase I are more likely to achieve profitable growth and less likely to fall into low-growth, low-profit tier in phase II.

WHY PROFITABILITY MATTERS
IN EMERGING MARKETS

In developed economies, profitability matters because it moves toward maximizing shareholder equity and interests. In classic management theory, the ultimate goal of a firm is to get the highest return for its shareholders, and the greatest source of return is profit. Companies embed return on assets, profit margins, and other profit metrics in their financial reports, and they use them as benchmarks for managerial performance and compensation.

The importance of profitability takes on a different significance in emerging markets. Unlike firms in developed economies, companies in emerging markets are not as beholden to shareholders. This fact doesn't make profitability any less important. In fact, the lack of shareholders often heightens the need for profitability, because more of the profits harvested from internal operations become the source for future growth. Even in cases where firms rely on external investments acquired through limited capital markets, raising money is a less effective tool in emerging markets due to their scarcity of reliable information and effective institutions. Potential investors avoid investments in businesses they don't know, partially due to fears that they might be misled by incorrect information.

Because of the risks attendant on external capital acquisitions, pursuing sales volume at the expense of profitability is a risk, sometimes even foolhardy, strategy. Consider the case of Aiduo, a Chinese manufacturer of video compact discs in the 1990s. Early in the decade, the video CD market in China was booming, and Aiduo was riding the wave of its initial success and making greater investments in marketing and advertising. In 1996, it paid 4.5 million RMB ($720,000), roughly one year's profit, to hire movie stars as brand ambassadors. Sales jumped to 1.6 billion RMB in 1997 from 200 million RMB the year before.[13] In 1998, the firm ratcheted up its marketing efforts even further, paying 210 million RMB for a five-second advertising slot on CCTV. And to grab even a larger market share from its competitors, Aiduo launched a price war on video CDs.

Aiduo had one strategy: grow bigger and bigger. It worked extremely well for a few years, but when market growth slowed, its profitability plummeted. Worse, because foreign firms controlled the core video CD technology, Aiduo and other domestic Chinese firms could not raise prices and continue to compete. By 1999, Aiduo could not repay the heavy debts it had accumulated during its rapid growth and its poorly timed price war. It declared bankruptcy in 1999—it took just four years to go from a superstar company to oblivion.

INTEGRATING PROFITABILITY WITH QUALIFIED SALES GROWTH

Why can firms that initially pursue profitability make the transition to high sales growth, while so few companies can move in the other direction? The answer lies in a firm's capacity to expand, but not necessarily as described by conventional theories of business growth. Mainstream thinking suggests that high-sales-growth firms succeed because they establish economies of scale and scope.[14] This strategy is common in relatively mature, commodity-focused industries, such as steel and cement. And it presumes that a prospective entrant has adequate resources to offset entry barriers.

In emerging markets, though, only a small portion of companies possess the resources to do this successfully. Even in commodity industries, these companies struggle to scale with their expansion. In some cases, state-owned enterprises have already capitalized on their first-mover advantage to establish market dominance. But even in markets not secured by the state-owned businesses, up-and-coming companies have to overcome underdeveloped institutions, which limit or raise the cost of outside resources that could support profitable growth.

As the first two demand-focused Four Cs show, the rough diamonds sidestepped the traditional barriers by successfully exploiting market niches and segments that market leaders had ignored or left unattended. Their success stemmed from the fact that they flew under the radar and could avoid unwanted competition. Moreover, industry incumbents tended to avoid investments in still-evolving segments because these moves would have required trade-offs on their higher-priority expansion strategies.

Timing proved to be a critical factor in entering these segments because rough diamonds had to invest in market development before demand had materialized. Rough diamonds were hardly meek in their approach, but they remained judicious and deliberate. Despite the risk, these companies believed bold moves today would put them in a better position to fend off entrants in the future. In this context, profits didn't become an afterthought. In fact, profit rose in importance because it provided the cushion against bumps in the road, dry powder to fend off potential entrants, and a source of capital for future expansion.

To be clear, though, sales and market share growth are important and necessary in both developed and emerging markets but for different reasons in emerging markets. First, high growth often signals stability and presages future success. It's not uncommon to see a flurry of government programs designed to boost growth through greater employment or tax revenues. Second, a larger company in an emerging market can funnel more funds into a smaller firm, serving as a sort of internal capital market in a manner similar to the Japanese *keiretsu* and the Korean *chaebol*.[15] And third, customers and citizens often view large companies as a critical institutional safeguard that can enforce legal and contractual terms to a degree that the country's public infrastructure might not reach.[16]

High sales growth in emerging markets is desired, but it comes with qualifications. For profitable growth, the goal is not solely sheer market dominance, although no firm would reject a strong market share. The goal is that the benefits and consequences of growth accrue not simply from the growth itself but from the company's expanding internal competencies as well. To the extent that already profitable firms can orient their strategy to capitalize on the benefits of greater sales and market share, they can attain much-coveted profitable growth as well.

PROFITABLE GROWTH THROUGH CORE COMPETENCIES

Profitable growth, sustained over time, relates directly to a company's ability to develop its core competencies (box 7.1). They are the key drivers of profit. Our study shows that rough diamonds consistently built on the competencies they drew from their deep knowledge of local markets and their operational excellence. And many of the same rough diamonds invested aggressively, but conscientiously, in research and development efforts that helped upgrade and expand on their existing competencies, an investment that positioned them for future growth.

Finally, our study shows that the sustainability of performance in emerging markets is more multifaceted than it's conventionally depicted. Sustained growth in these markets unquestionably depends on macroeconomic conditions, industrial evolution, and government policies that create future winners in global competition. But the ability of these high performers to experience enduring success will largely grow from their ability to achieve profitable growth over time.

Linyang Electronics, a manufacturer of smart electric meters, is an example of profitable growth through core

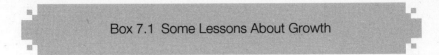

Box 7.1 Some Lessons About Growth

Top performers take different approaches to sustain their performance, but virtually all of them focus on building internal profits ahead of sheer market share. Yet sustained performance does not happen without the development of internal competencies. Successful companies typically pay heed to a similar set of directives to develop the internal competencies necessary to build sales and profit growth together.

Rapid Growth Does Not Guarantee High Profit

Although emerging markets are growing rapidly and provide opportunities for growth, firms should not blindly pursue rapid growth without considering how future profits can be funneled into new investments. Our results show that half the firms that initially pursued a sales-growth-oriented strategy eventually lost both sales and profits. To be sustainable, firms must develop the necessary competencies. Profits and competitive advantage are tied together — the horse pulling the cart instead of the other way around.

Becoming Vertically Integrated Is an Important Way to Achieve Sustainable Growth in Emerging Markets

In emerging markets, vertical integration is the single most important avenue for sustainable profitable growth. Vertical integration not only leads to firm expansion; it also reduces transaction costs. Efficiency results when firms can guarantee high product quality and timely delivery, keys to building competitive advantages. In our study, more than half of the rough diamonds vertically integrated. (Of course, a firm cannot continue to conduct vertical integration. After it has completed integrating its value chain and securing its control, it has to look to other strategies for expansion.)

"Do It Yourself" When Conducting Product Diversification

Selecting an appropriate entry mode influences the success rate of product diversification. Regardless of the type of product diversification, our research found that rough diamonds prefer the greenfield mode over M&A or joint ventures. In fact, greenfield investments account for more than 70 percent of product diversification strategies deployed by successful firms. Given the high transaction costs and low levels of trust and information about potential partners in emerging markets, it's safer to take a do-it-yourself approach to product diversification.

Leverage Relationships by Conducting Product Diversification Plans

Successful Chinese firms use their relationships as a key asset in diversification. Those with high relational capital are able to diversify into unrelated businesses more frequently, more rapidly, and more extensively than competing firms do. Moreover, they are able to adopt more diverse entry modes rather than relying solely on greenfield investments. Because relational capital is not confined to one particular business, its value can increase when firms use it broadly and repeatedly.

Develop a Strategic Plan for Local Partnerships

Multinational companies have to decide whether they should respond to local companies as direct competitors or strategic partners. As direct competitors, multinationals can employ two core strategies. First is to research a local competitor through the lines of their own growth strategies. Local firms that have successfully combined sales growth with high profits (profitable growth) are likely to be more formidable than firms pursuing one strategy or the other. Second, develop a systematic strategic program that focuses on local market assessment. In our study, top performers capitalized on the diversity of local markets, incorporating key local priorities and interests.

It is critical that as potential strategic partners, multinationals develop a contingency plan for a meaningful relationship with a new global player. A deep understanding of the top performers reveals the microfoundations of sustained growth, such as strategic intent, trade-offs between sales growth and profitability, and underpinning core competencies. Collectively, these foundations and trade-offs foreshadow the emerging rules of the game for global competition.

competencies. Linyang first enjoyed high growth due to the increasing demand for electric energy meters in most cities in China. During this period of soaring growth in its primary market, the firm continued to invest in other competitive advantages. It invested more than 5 percent of its revenue in

R&D each year, establishing research centers in several Chinese cities. All told, 12 percent of the company's employees are dedicated to R&D. Linyang also moved outside its own walls to participate in several national research projects. As a result, the firm owns sixty-one patents, eight software copyrights, and several nonpatent technologies.

All the while, it invested in its brand reputation. It put systems and people in place to ensure product quality throughout the value chain: from raw materials, to equipment, to employees, to finished products. Linyang's product-defect rate regularly runs far lower than the national standard. It supplemented that quality assurance with a quality feedback system that tracks its products over time. Linyang has always remained focused on profitability first, but it wasn't afraid to boldly channel those profits into qualified growth. Unsurprisingly, the company moved into the high-growth, high-profit category in the second five-year term of our study.

Cimento Itambé provides another excellent case study for profitable growth. The Brazilian cement manufacturer initially enjoyed high profits that resulted from its high-quality products, low costs, and close relationships with large customers. It built the first cement factory in Brazil and obtained the international ISO 9001 accreditation. It reduced costs by incinerating waste as a fuel source and has one of just six environmental permits in Brazil to do this. The fuel provides 15 percent of energy needed to run Itambé's ovens, and it can use the resulting ash as raw material for its cement. Moreover, the firm is selective in choosing its customers, seeking large clients that make quality products a priority. One-third of Brazil's total cement demand comes from large customers; for Itambé, that ratio is 70 percent.

All of these competitive advantages turn into large profits for the firm and then into future growth. Economies of scale are important in the cement industry, so Itambé has not stopped expanding. It steadily increased the capacity of its existing plant and invested in new one. Over the years, Cimento Itambé has maintained its leadership position in southern Brazil with a 16 percent market share in the region. *AH OR HL?*

The core competencies like those at Itambé and Linyang are generally praised, but they are not guaranteed moneymakers. Staking a position in new market niches is inherently risky. It requires bold action and visionary leadership—and, in many cases, creating and consolidating demand. In emerging markets, an especially wide gap can open between a company's goals and its ability to fulfill them. More than almost any other factor, the degree of that separation ultimately dictates a company's growth path. Rough diamonds bring their goals and abilities together to fuel high sales growth or high profit growth as dictated by the market and their strategy. Better yet, the rough diamonds bring both sales growth and profit together.

The next step is sustaining this profitable growth for the long haul.

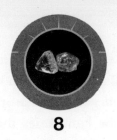

8

Hypergrowth

Can It Be Sustained?

There are two beliefs about growth that are well acclaimed in academic studies: first, that high growth cannot last forever; and second, it is more difficult to keep up the pace of growth when much of it has already taken place. The first speaks to natural limits of resources and human capital. As with all natural units that require sustained resources that are also limited, there is a cycle of reproduction, growth, and decay. Eventually, growth will approach its natural limit. The second speaks to the baseline in which growth is measured. In emerging and developing markets, growth will outstrip developed economies simply because there are more prodigious opportunities to grow and develop.

—SKOLKOVO Business School–Ernst & Young Institute
for Emerging Market Studies, *Rough Diamonds: The 4Cs
Framework for Sustained High Performance*

This chapter further addresses sustainability in emerging markets. While the meteoric growth of rough diamonds has boded well for emerging markets, their sustainability will depend on several factors: continued privatization; primary drivers, which directly bear on strategies, choices, actions, and consequences; and secondary drivers, including the unexpected consequences that result from a key event.

The term *hypergrowth* gets tossed around a lot, but we rarely hear it used to describe companies that post strong growth rates over a long period of time. The latest hot Silicon Valley hit goes into hypergrowth mode, but no one refers to hypergrowth when the same company has posted consistently strong sales growth a decade later. Yet when we look at the rough diamonds over the past ten years, it's hard to argue the term doesn't apply. Collectively, these companies posted average annual sales growth rates of roughly 43 percent across the decade we studied.

Those are remarkable growth rates, and it's reasonable to presume that such high rates cannot last permanently—any more than we'd expect more than a handful of the best Silicon Valley companies to keep doubling sales every year for that long. So how long can we expect the growth trajectory of the rough diamonds to continue at its current pace? And what factors might influence their ability to sustain this hypergrowth into the future? The second question helps answer the first. We have identified three primary factors that will have an impact on profitable growth over time: privatization in emerging markets, primary drivers that directly influence rough diamond strategies, and secondary or indirect drivers that alter the environment in which those strategic decisions are made.

PRIVATIZATION IN EMERGING MARKETS

The surge of privatization within the BRIC countries provided the fuel for a wave of entrepreneurial activity based on new business models. This sweeping transformation didn't happen at once, and it didn't take any standardized form in each of the four countries. And while it did spark the creation of some incredible companies in all the BRIC nations, including many of the rough diamonds, it's worth noting the unique characteristics in each.

Private firms did not exist in China until the economic reforms that started in 1978, but thousands of private enterprises have emerged since the country began moving toward a more market-oriented economy. In 1990, about 1.7 million people worked for private Chinese firms. That figure had skyrocketed to 86 million by 2009. Now, more than nine of every ten companies in China are private sector, and they employ 60 percent of the country's workers. The total output from private firms exceeds 50 percent of national GDP, embedding them as an integral component of China's economy (figure 8.1).

Russia experienced an even more radical history of privatization. From 1992 to 1994, a period of mass privatization in the country, 41 percent of the country's 120,000 large enterprises and half its small businesses hopped over to the private sector. About 20,000 joint stock companies were established. In the three years that followed the initial privatization boom, several of the country's most important enterprises sold through cash deals or auctions to employees, all to help close federal deficits. By the time 1997 had come and gone, privatization took on a more measured tone, with previously public enterprises going private on a case-by-case basis and through a regulated process.

As in China, private enterprises have become an important sector of the Russian economy. By the start of 2010, the country was home to more than 4 million private enterprises, about 84 percent of all firms (up from 63 percent in 1996). Similarly, these private firms employed 68 percent of the country's

FIGURE 8.1 Private Firms in China, 1998–2010

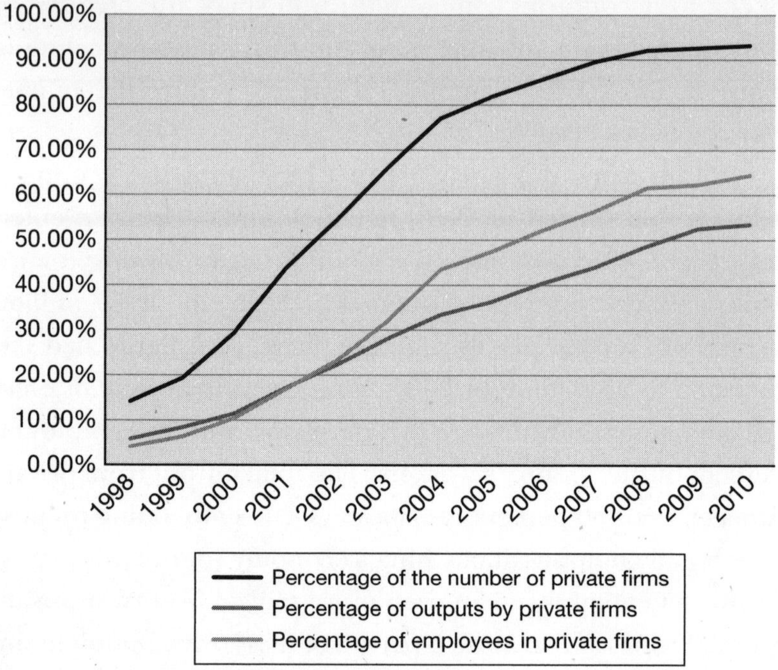

Source: *Chinese Statistical Yearbook*, various editions.

total employees in 2009, compared with 31 percent in 1992 (figure 8.2).

The privatization process in India and Brazil stretched over a much longer period than in China and Russia. In India, private firms accounted for 82.5 percent of the country's GDP in 1993–1994. That figure had ticked up to 86.9 percent in 2006–2007. Private firms dominate certain industries—for example, 97 percent of firms in the agricultural sector and 85 percent in manufacturing were private (figure 8.3).[1] Private firms in India contribute to around one third of the paid-up capital in the country. During these decades of growth, many private firms in India have transformed into large business groups. The

FIGURE 8.2 Private Firms in Russia, 2000–2009

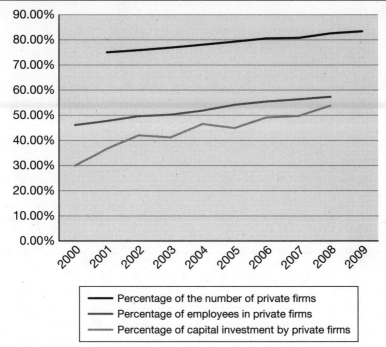

Source: *Russian Statistics Yearbook*, various editions.

most famous one is Tata Group, the largest private corporation in India, with interests in communications and information technology, engineering, materials, services, energy, consumer products, and chemicals. The Tata Group has operations in more than eighty countries across six continents, and its companies export products and services to eighty nations.

As in India, private firms in Brazil have long been an important part of the national economy. The early stages of privatization came largely in response to fiscal pressures in the early 1980s (about thirty-three firms were privatized before 1990). The trend escalated after 1990, due in large part to governmental policies enacted by the Collor (about fifteen firms),

FIGURE 8.3   Private Firms in India, 2001–2009

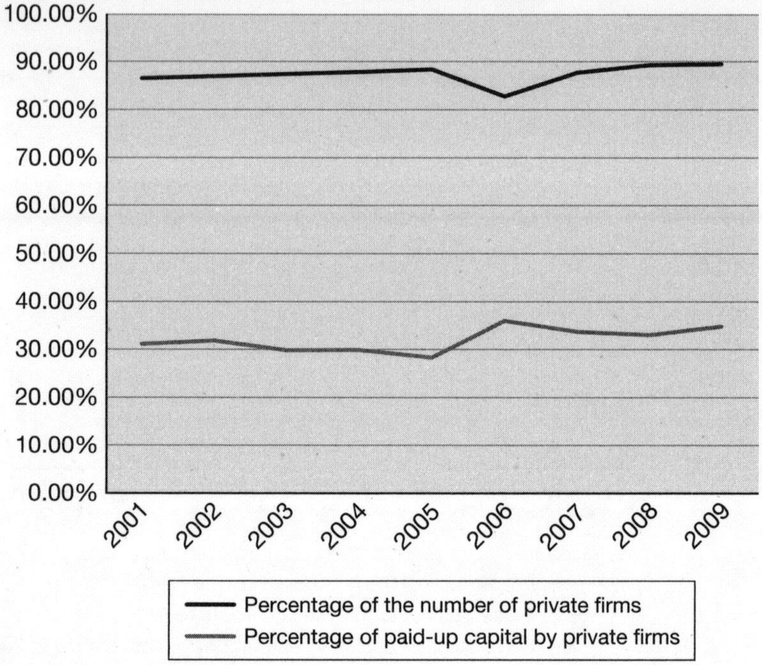

Percentage of the number of private firms
Percentage of paid-up capital by private firms

Source: Indian Statistics Yearbook, various editions.

Franco (about twenty-five firms), and Cardoso administrations (about eighty firms).[2] Around 80 percent of firms in Brazil are private firms, and these firms employed more than 80 percent of employees between 2001 and 2011 (figure 8.4). In April 2011, the private sector in Brazil employed almost 13.4 million people, accounting for 77.3 percent of its total workforce.[3]

Despite the dynamism associated with privatization, it does not come without challenges, including for upstart firms in an era of late development. Since the 1980s, globalization, market liberalization, and a growing middle class have prompted the need for greater integration with the global economy.[4] These forces gave rise to early market leaders. Many of those early

FIGURE 8.4   Private Firms in Brazil, 2001–2011

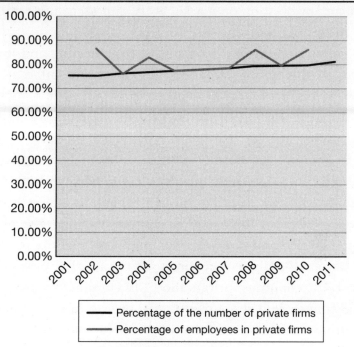

Source: Brazil Statistics Yearbook, various editions.

leaders in China and Russia were owned or supported by the state. In Brazil and India, most of the early leaders had the benefit of a long-standing historical legacy.

The incumbents didn't sit still during the growth spurt of the early 2000s. Most of them moved aggressively to bolster their market presence and competitive position, often by expanding exports to both developed and developing countries. In that environment, new private sector entrants had to reconfigure their value chain, creating differentiation at some point on which it could compete with the incumbents. Even today, new and upstart firms have to remain keenly in tune with market signals that could suggest industry developments or favorable changes in government policies. And, of course, they would have to align any decision on market entry with their investment in internal resources.

These windows of opportunity can be fleeting and intractable, so the timing of moves into local and international markets becomes a critical element of any firm's strategy. Entering a market prematurely exposes the enterprising firm to fledgling and inchoate market segments or niches, which might require significantly more investment than hoped or planned for. (Moreover, they face potential retaliation from incumbents.) But entering too late or doing nothing as competitors stake out their market position and reap the profits from their decision can limit a company's competitive position.

Despite the higher percentage of private enterprises in all four BRIC countries, privatization will continue to spark new opportunities and support sustained growth in those nations. The trend toward privatization is not inexorable, but it has not stopped rising. And that in turn will spawn new generations of exemplary firms, most likely including a generation of future rough diamonds. Nevertheless, increased privatization alone is not any guarantee of success. While this bodes well for current and future rough diamonds, our research uncovered one important caveat: these future firms will have to be able to capitalize on windows of opportunity and build core competencies in the process much as the current rough diamonds have done.

DIAGNOSING SUSTAINED GROWTH FROM PRIMARY DRIVERS

Academic studies usually break down the limits to growth in two ways. The first way argues that growth cannot last forever. The exhaustion of natural and human resources takes precedence as the inevitable cycle of birth, growth, and decay marches on. Eventually growth approaches its natural limit. The second argument speaks to the baseline by which growth is measured. In emerging and developing markets, growth will outstrip developed economies simply because there are more prodigious opportunities to grow and develop. Over time, sheer size and saturation make growth rates harder and harder to maintain.

Contemporary strategic management theories have introduced some nuance into this discussion. In this view, companies face dynamic conditions—what we call primary drivers—that have a direct impact on their ability to sustain profitable growth. In the acclaimed five forces model formulated by Harvard University strategy guru Michael Porter, changes in rivalry, suppliers, buyers, substitute products, and entry barriers collectively define the overall attractiveness of any given industry.[5] Without strategic attention to them, the five forces can drive any industry back toward its "floor rate of return," or the minimal return on invested capital it would generate in a theoretical environment of perfect competition. Porter's argument gained greater significance when former Intel Corp. chairman Andy Grove introduced his idea of a strategic inflection point: changes in any one of the five forces that exceed a predetermined threshold thus significantly change the basis of competition and rivalry.[6]

Within our Four Cs framework, we defined a set of primary drivers as the underlying industry conditions that directly bear on the strategies, choices, actions, and consequences that rough diamonds experience. For a large portion of the rough diamonds, our primary drivers added nuance to Porter's five forces. To be sure, some of the rough diamonds excelled in some of the more attractive industries with higher barriers to entry or higher sales growth—Jinglong in solar and semiconductor, and Sitronics in telecom, and Bombay Rayon in textiles, for example. And for these companies, the five forces were instructive. However, the bulk of the rough diamonds play in maturing industries that aren't as robust. Among these industries, our study showed that the ability to sustain a competitive advantage—through cost and differentiation advantages or by establishing a defensible market niche—has a more important influence on strategic decisions over time.[7] Most of the rough diamonds developed cost or differentiation advantages, particularly in manufacturing operations (i.e., operational excellence). More broadly, though, rough diamonds had an almost unique ability to craft operational excellence from a variety of strategies. Moreover, they excelled at the strategic implementation of those strategies.

Ultimately our results showed that the rough diamonds' competitive positions were relatively secure and defensible over the ten-year study period, despite the few barriers to entry or the moderate growth of their industries. In other words, sustained success goes beyond merely developing a favorable competitive position; it means sustaining that position through excellent execution over time, especially when evidence suggests that the industry characteristics might not be as attractive as other sectors.

We offer one final note on the primary drivers: while companies that fully integrated each of the Four Cs tended to post higher performance over time, the results were not uniform. Every one of the rough diamonds employed the first two of the Four Cs, capitalizing on opportunities and creating new markets. But the extent to which they adopted the remaining two of the Four Cs—crafting operation excellence and cultivating profitable growth—varied from company to company, as did their results.

ASSESSING SUSTAINED GROWTH USING SECONDARY DRIVERS

Changes in the primary drivers tend to grab the most attention, and perhaps rightfully so. But they don't tell the whole story of sustained growth in emerging markets. To get the full picture, one must examine the nascent, indirect conditions and events that so influence the primary drivers. Such conditions and events are what we call secondary drivers—the unexpected consequences that emanate or follow from a major event. These are the aftershocks following an earthquake or the side effects of a drug. While such events might be anticipated, their timing, magnitude, and ultimate consequences can rarely be known in advance. Even so, we can safely ascribe three characteristics to describe these secondary drivers: they derive from both internal and external changes, they closely interact with primary drivers, and their consequences can have a more intense impact than the primary ones.

Because decisions relating to primary and secondary drivers are equivocal and not easy to untangle, we can use the timing of the transformative event to differentiate them. For example, a government decision to reverse a policy of exports in favor of import substitution might provide a brand-new opportunity for erstwhile firms to engage in local production. Similarly, the weeding out of marginal firms that occurs during an industry shakeout can strengthen strong and competitive firms. As we discussed earlier in this book, the confluence of government policies with industry evolution often creates favorable conditions for rough diamonds to enter previously unattended market niches and segments.

Although the secondary drivers can seem obvious in retrospect, they often are congealed in evolving political, economic,

TABLE 8.1 Classification of Primary and Secondary Drivers

4Cs for Sustained High Performance	Key RD Strategic Components	Primary Drivers	Secondary Drivers
Capitalizing on late development	Visionary, entrepreneurial, and market orientation	Privatization New government policies Industry transitions	Accelerated pressures from globalization and market liberalization
Creating inclusive market niches and segments	Deep awareness of local markets and demand	Changes in demand and consumption Growth of market segments	Rising middle class Improved institutional environments
Crafting operational excellence	Variety of ways to develop core competencies	Value creation arising from integrated logistics, supply chain management, measures, and management systems	Success of delayed maturity New competition
Cultivating profitable growth	Leveraging local competencies to profitable growth trajectories	Benefits derived from access to domestic and international markets	Accelerated internationalization Sequential learning Subsidiary management

and institutional contexts and therefore they can be hard to identify. However, our research showed a general correlation between each of the Four C phases, the strategies they entailed, and the primary and secondary drivers that attended them (table 8.1).

To help better identify the myriad secondary drivers that influence strategy and sustained success, we developed a set of key questions that, like a detective's investigation, can help lead to these often subtle factors:

- *Will globalization and market liberalization continue to have an impact on government policy and industry evolution?* Globalization is an unfolding process, not an end state. The immediacy of information exchange facilitated by the Internet and social media adds pressure to provide similar products and services to consumers around the world. Moreover, there is increased pressure for emerging countries to liberalize and open up their markets in order to resolve the trade imbalances that result from their burgeoning exports to developed countries. But liberalization is a double-edged sword, and rough diamonds have to carefully assess whether future policies will facilitate or obstruct their intended development.

- *Will the socioeconomic rise of consumers continue to transform previously neglected market segments into viable and lucrative niches?* A rising middle class ensures more purchasing power for all types of goods, not just luxurious high-tech items. Other sectors, such as food, personal household items, clothing, and transportation, also transform as demand patterns for the emerging middle class begin to resemble those of developed countries. This demand transformation helps explain why rough diamonds have been able to capitalize on consumers' newly found purchasing power as they created and consolidated overlooked or forgotten market segments. In just China alone, estimates for the emerging middle class range from 100 million to 247 million people, with similar growth trends materializing in India, Russia, and Brazil as well.[8] Ernst & Young's own projections are equally optimistic: between now and 2030, the number of people in the global middle class will grow from 1.8 billion to 4.9 billion. The majority will live in Asia and other rapid-growth markets.[9] The growth of the middle-class sector, along with its rising purchasing power, underpins the market niches by strengthening demographic bonds, aggregating demand, and increasing consumption.

• *How will improved institutional environments transform the viability of producer and consumer sectors?* An increasing number of economists, including Ha-Joon Chang, Joseph Stiglitz, Herman Daly, and Sixto Roxas, have started to argue that growth is not the same as development, and for the most part, they are right.[10] However, it is equally misleading to argue that growth has no part of development at all. The two are tightly interrelated because of the secondary effects they generate, including the improvement of institutional environments. With higher income, individuals invest in technologies that bring them closer together, obviating traditional hurdles to access and product information. With aggregated demand, consumer preferences are better defined, providing important clues for entry and market development. More refined consumer targets provide important information for eventual price points, market segmentation, and competitive benchmarking. Collectively, growth and development are promoted by information and facilitated by markets, resulting in improved institutions that can accrue to higher rough diamond performance.

• *Can the rough diamonds continue to delay maturity through differentiation strategies?* For the time being, some rough diamonds in specialized market niches are able to charge premium prices because their consumers are willing to pay for differentiated features. The extent to which firms differentiate, combined with the corresponding power of a rising middle class that can pay more for products and services, can effectively delay product maturation. This can be sustained for as long as new market niches appear and growth in the consumer base continues, but lower costs, more saturated markets, and greater manufacturing efficiencies can quickly accelerate industry maturation.

- *How will rough diamonds respond to new competitors?* The progression of industry maturation will switch the playbook from brand differentiation to price competition. With ensuing competition based on prices and commodities, new competitors will introduce uncertainty in the market, and rivalries will intensify. As in developed countries, emerging market mavericks can bring in new and unexpected forms of competition. To the extent that rough diamonds are secure with their core competencies and able to reap extended benefits from scale and scope economies, they stand a good chance of maintaining their advantages and competitive positions—and thereby sustain profitable growth. However, long-term success is never assured, especially when new domestic and international competitors can enter the market and the government and other external factors can change the rules of the game. It is critical that rough diamonds monitor industry developments and potential rivals.

- *Can rough diamonds continue to leverage their strengths in both domestic and international growth strategies?* Success in the local market does not guarantee success in global markets. The key challenge for rough diamonds is how well they can compete with the international strategies of other global players. New players have adopted different growth trajectories based on timing, sequential entries, and learning from previous experiences. Unlike previous years, the relationship between headquarters and its subsidiaries is vastly different. New competencies are based on rapid local learning, multiple strategic alliances, decision making using virtual or software-based communication channels, and the effective use of listening posts and other methods of gathering information and intelligence.[11]

Because secondary drivers are in a continuing state of evolution, assessing their occurrences can be daunting. What binds them together are their links to the primary transformative event that sparked them. The pattern of sequential after-effects might be hard to predict in terms of both timing and consequences, but rough diamonds need to identify and assess the primary and secondary drivers to sustain profitable growth over the long term.

The environments that generate the drivers vary from company to company and, especially, from country to country. We turn our attention next to the national differences among the BRIC countries and the impact these can have on the rough diamonds' sustained performance.

9

National Differences

A Tale of Four Countries

In all, while RDs share a common kernel for success (the Four Cs), the underlying context that drives their successes are deeply rooted in country history, traditions, and legacies. In part, their success is derived from continued high economic growth in each country. But it is the combination of country factors that provide the basis that defines the specific entrepreneurial spirit and ensuing strategies of successful RDs in this study.

> —SKOLKOVO Business School–Ernst & Young Institute for Emerging Market Studies, *Rough Diamonds: The Four Cs Framework for Sustained High Performance*

Whereas the previous chapters have underscored the shared competencies of rough diamonds, this chapter probes into basic country-specific differences among these companies. The different historical, institutional, and cultural factors in each of the BRIC nations have an influence on the way firms in those countries develop. China's rough diamonds leverage their relationships, Brazilian firms focus on their brand legacies, Russian companies highlight their entrepreneurial competencies, and Indian companies build around their legacy of innovation.

When we reviewed all the data and pored over all the secondary information, interviews, and consultations with emerging market experts, we could not help but notice the unique, country-specific factors that jumped out at us. Some of them jump out from the data themselves.

Specifically, as discussed in chapter 1, we found that Chinese rough diamonds outperformed top 500 firms in virtually every output category during the study period: efficiency, sales growth, return on assets, profit margin, and market share. Russian rough diamonds also posted strong sales growth and profit margins but they tended to have lower market share figures than top 500 firms. However, Indian rough diamonds, although showing strong performance across the board, had the strongest market positions with almost four times the market share of the rough diamonds in other BRIC countries. In Brazil, rough diamonds performed substantially better than top 500 firms in profitability and market share but they were marginally better in growth rate reflecting market maturity compared to other countries.

Brazil's rough diamonds were older than companies at large. Their Indian and Russian counterparts were younger than the field of businesses in their countries. China's rough diamonds were all around the same age, although they were younger than their counterparts in the other BRIC countries. (Although China and Russia started privatizing businesses in the 1980s, more of the Russian rough diamonds had longer histories as state-owned companies.)

We could fill volumes with all the variations among the rough diamonds in one country or the next, but as we looked through the data, we could not escape the fact that a small number of rather specific factors in each country had an

TABLE 9.1 Relative Importance of Key Success Factor

	China	Russia	India	Brazil
Early success				
Access to raw materials	**	*	**	*
Access to technology	**	*	***	**
Niche market	**	***	**	***
Entrepreneurs	***	***	**	**
Core competence				
Integrated logistics management	***	***	**	***
Customer orientation	***	***	***	**
Quality control	**	**	***	**
Management system	**	***	***	***
Innovation	***	*	***	***
Growth management				
Product diversification	***	*	*	**
Internationalization	***	*	**	**

outsized influence on the companies that developed there. As we compared our data-driven findings with the qualitative information we had compiled, we could compare the relative importance of several critical resources on the rough diamonds (table 9.1). And from that we boiled down to the single greatest distinguishing factor in each of the BRIC countries.

CHINA: MOBILIZING RELATIONAL CAPITAL FOR GROWTH

Chinese rough diamonds excel at entrepreneurship, supply chain management, customer orientation, innovation, and growth management. The single factor that binds all of those together is relationships. Popularly known as *guanxi*, this trait derives from the rough diamonds' strong bonds with a broad range of customers, suppliers, shareholders, and partners. But more fundamental, *guanxi* also arises from a cultural orientation in Chinese society that cherishes strength from close connections.[1]

Because relationships and connections become the gears of China's economic and social exchanges, they supplement the country's weak formal institutions. This proves critical not only in the initial stages, but in all other phases of a company's development. Relationships facilitate scaling up of operations, expansions, and leveraging competencies to expand internationally—all essential for sustaining market niches and growth.

China's history of state control heightens the premium on relationships. Because of their legacy of state or collective ownership, the Chinese rough diamonds put great effort into formalizing their ownership. Even in the many cases when the government did not invest in these firms, public aid is often critical to establish a solid ownership structure. Relationships play on a critical role in this process (box 9.1).

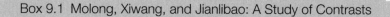

Box 9.1 Molong, Xiwang, and Jianlibao: A Study of Contrasts

Molong was originally a state-owned enterprise. From 1987 to 1997, with extensive effort from managers and help from local government, the firm finished the privatization process, which granted the managers 60 percent of the shares. The smooth privatization not only gave managers the autonomy to run the company, it motivated them to work hard. Similarly, Xiwang Group, a collectively owned enterprise, finished its ownership transformation in 2002 by issuing shares to individuals, mostly the villagers, which was seen at the time to be an innovative initiative. It was not easy to accomplish this, and many storied Chinese firms have failed in the past as a result of this transformation. Jianlibao, a famous brand of athletic beverages in the 1990s, was a celebrated case of failure. Because of conflicts with the local government, Jianlibao's founder, Jingwei Li, could not privatize his company as he expected. The firm was then sold to an outsider, which led to its precipitous decline. Jingwei Li was later charged with corruption and sentenced to fifteen years in prison.

Relationships also take on vital importance in building distribution networks and innovation capabilities. Chemical fertilizer maker Shandong Kingenta sold primarily to small farmers geographically dispersed throughout China. To reach such a spread-out customer base, it cooperated with the marketing center at China Post's, the largest postal service firm in China, press center. By tapping into the post's network of resources, it could deliver its products directly to customers, which cut costs and boosted brand value. To strengthen the program and brand image even further, Kingenta backed its controlled-release fertilizers with a training program for new farmers.

In 2008, it took its marketing a step further. It created a new program, advertised as "stronghold plus agricultural service," which established a "stronghold" team of three or four professionals from various backgrounds who collectively offered advice, products, and services for a three- or four-county area. Today Kingenta has more than one hundred professionals and a fleet of three hundred cars to provide scientific fertilization techniques to farmers for free. It hosts a series of agricultural services every year, which farmers welcome. Its marketing network has expanded to more than twenty-five provinces, and its market share has risen to over 50 percent. It leveraged its relationships with the China Post and other partners to ultimately establish direct relationships with its customers.

While Kingenta tapped into its network of relationships to expand its primary business, many of China's rough diamonds have used the same sorts of connections to diversify into a range of new businesses. In fact, the relationship-based business environment in the country might explain why Chinese firms tend to take a more aggressive approach to diversification. Whenever a firm wants to change its product or geographical scope, it has to apply and register with the corresponding government agencies within thirty days after the decision has been made. This registration and application process usually takes a considerable amount of time and involves multiple government agencies.

In addition to these strict regulations, certain industries can be classified as an "authorized business." The licensing process for this certification creates significant barriers to entry for upstart companies, but our secondary research revealed a remarkable ability of rough diamonds to expand despite these barriers. They do so by relying on their relationships. Risun tapped into its local government connections to help gather the resources that helped pave the way to its rough diamond status today. A coking company in Hebei Province, Risun used its connections to tie its fortunes with local government interests. The company was, after all, a large taxpayer. Led by CEO Xuegang Yang, a former government official, the company received preferential policies in land, taxation, resources, information, water distribution, and many other privileges. The government of Xingtai expropriated seven hundred acres of land for the company to establish the Risun & Xingtai industrial park. It invested almost 12 billion RMB ($1.93 billion) to build Risun Avenue, Risun Road, a set of logistics channels, railway lines, and a 110 kilovolt substation in the industrial park.

As Risun and a host of other companies in other industries prove, these vital relationships are not limited by bureaucracy or lines of business, and the Chinese rough diamonds use them fully. In fact, we would posit that the success of these firms would not occur—certainly not to the same extent, anyway—without a broad and deep network of relationships with government, suppliers, partners, customers, and beyond.

BRAZIL: CAPABILITY-BASED
BRAND ADVANTAGE

More than rough diamonds in the other BRIC countries, those in Brazil leveraged their brand legacy. Brazilian rough diamonds tend to have longer histories than their counterparts in the other three countries. Rather than take that advantage for granted, these companies have enhanced their value by differentiating their brands from those of competitors—whether through quality, innovation, price, or other factors. They used their brands to boost their product value, something difficult for competitors to match, and they did so relentlessly. Brand building, after all, takes time and a series of dedicated efforts.

The history of the Brazilian economy has provided multiple opportunities for brand building among the country's rough diamonds. The industrialization of Brazil, for example, began during the turn of the twentieth century, shortly after the founding of the republic of Brazil in 1889. Because Brazil was unscathed by the two world wars, its business sphere has enjoyed a long period of uninterrupted development. As a result, rough diamonds in Brazil had a long, mostly smooth environment in which to develop and strengthen their brands. As they combined that with increasingly advanced managerial capabilities and downstream competencies, they pushed their brand strength into various markets and geographies.

Yet what stood out in our study was the remarkable ability of the Brazilian rough diamonds to develop the core of their brand: their brand identity. Because customers so readily equate a brand entity with the firm itself, good branding almost invariably leads to high customer loyalty. Many of Brazil's rough diamonds have engendered that high-quality brand value and treasured brand loyalty (box 9.2).

Box 9.2 Arezzo's Brand Legacy

In the 1970s, the Birman family, sensing that Brazilian fashion had gone stale, sought to connect with the broad influence of European fashion, particularly Italian trends. It created Arezzo to tap into everything chic for footwear. The combination of Arezzo's skills as a footwear manufacturer and retailer took the market by surprise and quickly built a mass following. The company eventually turned its focus to the high-end market and opened its first flagship store on Oscar Freire Street, an important national and international design district in São Paulo.

Because the market for high-end footwear had gone largely neglected for so long, Arezzo could establish its dominance quickly. It hasn't let the brand languish in the decades since. In an interview, Arezzo's top managers credited its commitment to a highly flexible business model as the key to its sustained success. "The company buys the finished product, about 85 percent, adjusts speed to demand, and develops and monitors suppliers," they said. "Since the distribution strategy has three well-developed channels: our own stores, multi-brand stores, and franchises . . . the brand is highly concentrated in Arezzo franchises."

The same firms used their experience to keep building out the brand as well, pushing core messages out through marketing and partner channels. Esmaltec, for example, used television, magazine, and newspaper ads to increase broad brand awareness of its appliances. But it also pushed deeper brand penetration through strong relationships with Brazil's large home appliance chains, such as Casas Bahia, that would promote its brand and products. Natura took another tack that fits the cosmetic industry beautifully: it held a beauty contest to raise its visibility and brand value. At points of sale, the company employs a large group of consultants who can share the company's vision of beauty inspired by nature, as well as its social and environmental causes.

That personal touch is common throughout the Brazilian rough diamonds, which know that establishing brand identity begins with excellent customer service and experience. Like any other good equipment company, Schulz focuses on all phases of its product development, from the first designs of its products to the final supplies. The company, which makes air and gas compressors, takes that a step further, offering its customers a network of services designed to solicit their feedback at every level of production and immediately meet any requirements they have. Its network might seem like overkill to less successful companies, but Schulz's work with customers from pre- to postsale with technical assistance, opens channels of communication with the process developers, and careful follow-up of each productive stage ensures that customers have the highest priority.

RUSSIA: ENTREPRENEURIAL LEADERSHIP FOR GROWTH

Russia's market liberalization in the early 1990s opened the door for the emergence of high-performing, well-managed private enterprises. Those firms, including the rough diamonds, originated from two distinctively different historical backgrounds: privatized state-owned enterprises and new entrepreneurial ventures. The privatized companies differed from similar companies in China because the Russian firms had existed for years. (Many of the Chinese companies were created from scratch as the country developed its private sector.) The Russian enterprises had historically high market shares thanks to their existence as largely monopolistic state-owned entities.

This level of market dominance provided them a natural advantage over new entrepreneurial ventures, which had to seek out market niches to gain a foothold.

The Russian rough diamonds were mostly born, or reborn, as private firms in the mid- to late 1990s while their markets were still disoriented and competitive. In that environment, the first phase of their growth focused on building market competitiveness, usually by increasing scale to gain a cost advantage or establishing brand saturation across markets. As they secured a competitive advantage in their market niches, they started to pursue regional and product diversification. Even as they looked to spread their wings, the Russian rough diamonds typically stayed close to their familiar origins.

Still, these usually well-educated, experienced, and well-connected founders had to rely heavily on their entrepreneurship to overcome the long Russian legacy of state-owned operations. They excelled at adopting new technological skills for new market opportunities. They forged strong managerial systems and shared values that led to sustained high performance over the last decade. And as visionaries, they relentlessly sought new opportunities in the domestic market, implementing their strategies with zeal and passion. Collectively these entrepreneurial traits enabled their early success and laid the foundation for developing related core competences in manufacturing and marketing (box 9.3).

Reflecting this success, Standard & Poor's gives several of the Russian rough diamonds high marks for governance. In fact, WBD established an exemplary record of high S&P ratings for transparency, openness, and oversight processes—unusual and atypical among companies in Russia. Along with its commitment to developing human resources and its high-quality workplace, the beverage company's operational and financial

Box 9.3 MLVZ: Doing Things Differently But the Right Way

MLVZ differentiated itself from competitors by adhering to a business model that avoided many of the traditional business practices and cultural influences. Historically a successful liquor business was built on a foundation of marketing and distribution. But as a relatively late entrant, MLVZ management placed higher emphasis on integrating and promoting a modern business culture of entrepreneurship, freedom of choice, and accountability. The other drivers behind this enterprising model included a strong corporate culture and processes to rapidly identify market trends, demand changes, and the need for supply chain modification.

transparency catapulted it to the list of most admired companies in both Russia and the international investment community.

This growing legacy of strong and visionary leadership lies at the root of the new breed of rough diamonds in Russia—a group that will continue to play a strong role in establishing modern management systems and supportive corporate cultures. They are both providing and fueling the broader push for visionary leadership at the upper echelons and participatory decision making at the operational levels. To be clear, upper-level strategic decisions are still made authoritatively, consistent with Russian culture, but these do not obscure a rising trend toward the involvement of other levels in critical decision making.

Raisa Demina, Velkom's director, exemplifies this new trend, and the Agricultural Business and Food Production Committee honored her as businesswoman of the year in 2010 for her efforts. The charismatic founder of Sady Pridonya,

Andrey Smokhin, used his deep understanding of the industry and his company to build strong connections with key stakeholders and the government, which was integral to his firm's success. Since the mid-1990s, WBD founder David Iakobachvili has advised government leaders on his approach to business and his vision of a more interactive management and organizational structure.

The Russian rough diamonds were launched by visionary leaders with a deep understanding of their businesses, but also with a keen eye toward new trends in the workplace, the need for strong external networks, and relentless pursuit of a strategic vision. Today, their strong managerial capabilities, focused on culture, leadership, governance, and flexible operations, are taking their long-standing entrepreneurial drive and pushing it to new levels of profitable growth.

INDIA: STRATEGICALLY MANAGED INNOVATION FOR GROWTH

When the raj license control era, or the time in which burgeoning licenses and regulations were needed to set up and manage a business in India, ended in 1990, Indian private firms capitalized on new opportunities in sectors that were previously state regulated. The rough diamonds, in particular, proved visionary in identifying market niches in which they could apply their internally developed capabilities and technologies they obtained from abroad. While most Indian rough diamonds remained family-controlled organizations, the families brought in and developed highly capable professional management teams that acquired expertise in innovative product and process technologies. More than in the other three BRIC countries, these Indian firms combined a traditional, family-controlled organization with the most modern technologies and business practices—all without compromising a management system based on a strong culture and human resources.

Traditional Indian companies that did not appreciate the synergy between technology and human capital fell behind during the new market orientation of the 1990s, exemplifying the stagnation of the government-directed, prereform era. While most companies struggled with outdated technologies and inefficiencies, rough diamonds became first movers in new markets, almost always employing innovative products and foreign technologies. Their systemic and well-executed strategies not only underpinned their operations in the 1990s; they helped them evolve into the innovative high-performance rough diamonds of the 2000s.

These companies also followed a carefully managed growth path by sticking to their primary businesses in domestic and international expansion. Whereas Chinese rough diamonds built on their relationships to expand more broadly, their Indian counterparts built success on a foundation of innovation and technical strengths within key industries. The Indian companies' consideration of balanced risk tempered their quest for unrelated diversification, leading them to higher sustained value from their core strengths and innate technological skills.

Titan, a market leader in watches, was the first to create a market for quartz technology. Parekh used its technical prowess and operational strengths to jump ahead in aluminum packaging, and Sudhir did the same with small power generator markets. In each case, though, innovation was merely a first step; each company also had to recognize the hidden potential of overlooked or untapped market niches (the first of the Four Cs). Especially in India, the rough diamonds' entrepreneurial and innovative insights led them to explore and subsequently enter niche markets in various sectors. This rich experience with the marketplace, combined with technological, organizational, and innovation prowess, made their early success and market leadership possible (box 9.4).

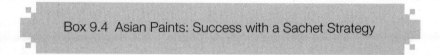

Box 9.4 Asian Paints: Success with a Sachet Strategy

Asian Paints is generally known for capitalizing on the governmental policy of import substitution. Even so, its success was also based on its ability to quickly understand an untapped market and reach out to retailers directly with smaller containers of its paint. This departure from large to smaller containers was quite new to the market but had unearthed a need that had remained unmet. Asian Paints' bold venture helped expand the market in volume and customer use, in effect consolidating the niche. Such innovative ventures have maintained the company's growth over more than a half-century of operations. In the words of P. M. Murty, its CEO, "Most of the time proactively tapping unidentified opportunities makes way for successful business. Finding niches and customizing product offering to meet the unmet needs of its customers helped Asian Paints gain market share early in its business cycle."

To be sure, the ability to identify a market niche in the midst of a sweeping market reformation is not a straightforward task, and it comes with high risk. But as they established an initial foothold, the Indian rough diamonds increasingly cultivated market-based innovation to drive their growth. These innovations often were driven by their workers who had new ideas. Every rough diamond is equipped with a comprehensive and sophisticated personnel development system that nurtures innovation.

Our research found that Indian rough diamonds put an especially high premium on the development of personnel, a priority that often led to strong market advantages and sustained profitable growth. In describing Marico, the Indian beauty and wellness company, Harsh Mariwala, its CEO, described its advantages:

> It is difficult for the competition to imitate Marico's core competence, as it is now engrained in the culture of the organization and has taken years of experimentation and over-investment in building enabling practices to strengthen the sources of these competencies . . . The success of "Parachute" brand in nipping the threat from its competitor "Nihar" in the year 2000 shows the strength of Marico's focus in its areas of core competence, [which] the company has identified as branding and customer orientation, distribution, innovation and cost management. The company is well placed to nix existential threats from its competition and grow at a rapid pace given its excellence in operating around its areas of core competence.

Innovation

Today some of India's rough diamonds are recognized as leading global knowledge centers because of their advanced innovation capabilities and facilities. They responded to market uncertainties arising from short product life cycles and intense competition by building superior and continuous innovation capabilities. At Thermax, for example, a customer-focused R&D structure helped the company to come up with solutions that eventually shaped market responses across the Indian energy sector. When the world suffered the shock of rocketing oil prices in the 1970s, Thermax introduced a coal-fired boiler that eventually helped Indian industries shift from their dependence on oil. By the 1980s and 1990s, Thermax was extending its fuel flexibility even further with products that used biomass and industrial waste as fuel for generating energy.

Its innovative solutions continue to produce widespread contributions across many industries. "The competitive advantage that sets Thermax apart from competition is our knowledge," said M. S. Unnikrishnan, the company's CEO. "Our unparalleled knowledge base in heat and mass transfer, combustion engineering, water and waste management technologies is essential to our business. Our dream is to become an R&D hub for the country and create the expertise to be shared with the rest of the world."

Human Capital and External Networks

Vijai Electronicals (VEL), a dominant player in India's transformer industry, enhanced its operational and technical strength through strategic technical collaborations with eminent world leaders in the industry, including Westinghouse (United States), Daihan (Japan), and M&C (Germany). Following its motto of "adherence to the customer's specifications," VEL developed some of the world's most innovative transformer technologies, including a transformer with the world's highest voltage rating.

Amtek developed some of the strongest internal capabilities in the India auto parts sector through both heavy internal R&D investments and work with Italy's Teksid. Today Amtek is one of the largest manufacturers of cylinder blocks in India and the only Indian casting company to use cutting-edge thin-wall technology. Its continuous upgrading of innovation capabilities helped it align with market changes and attain high annual growth and annual profit throughout the decade.

These and the other Indian rough diamonds have compiled a long list of innovations, but our research found they also supplement those efforts with continual and vital process improvements. Among all the rough diamonds, their early commitment to a total quality management system, which is relatively intractable and difficult to imitate, was crucial. These companies institutionalized quality management throughout their organizations and their entire value chains. And they all maintain a quality audit team to ensure that these high-quality management practices continue. It's a commitment that starts from the top, a management echelon that has embraced both indigenous skills and technological and business process advances from abroad.

COMMONALITIES AND DIFFERENCES

No matter which BRIC country they call home and no matter the long national histories and cultures that have shaped them, the rough diamonds all share the Four Cs as a common kernel for success. That plays out across different underlying contexts that influence the course of success. While their success is driven in part by continued high growth in each BRIC country, the different histories, traditions, and legacies still play out in different ways. In the end, it is this rich combination of country-level factors that provides the variety that colors the entrepreneurial spirit and the strategies of successful rough diamonds in this study.

As much as they have in common, each country and each rough diamond has its own unique characteristics. Outside companies and observers can learn much from both the commonalities and the differences.

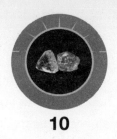

10

Responding to Rough Diamonds

Implications and Recommendations

> The global rules of the game must take into account the prospective late entrants into the global economy. If a continuous stream of new players defines the contours of competition, then attention should not be focused as intently on stable rules of the game, but on how these rules are constantly evolving.
>
> —SKOLKOVO Business School–Ernst & Young Institute for Emerging Market Studies, *Rough Diamonds: The 4Cs Framework for Sustained High Performance*

What impact will the rough diamonds have on the BRIC and global markets and the companies that compete against them? We offer six recommendations and implications: (1) rethink the rules of the game, (2) local is the new normal, (3) reduce ethnocentric tendencies, (4) recognize that some conventional beliefs about emerging markets no longer apply, (5) develop a contingency plan for strategic partnerships with rough diamonds, and (6) current and future rough diamonds signal the sustained growth of emerging markets.

The emergence of rough diamonds is reshaping markets, business practices, and national economies. We used a rigorous process to develop a list of just seventy of these exemplary firms, but many more companies have established themselves as a powerful influence in their industries and countries. And if we were to go through this process again in a decade or two, we almost certainly would have a lot of new companies that would join the ranks of rough diamonds.

As these companies maintain their profitable growth patterns, they undoubtedly will have an increasing influence not only in their own industries and domestic markets but across business segments and throughout the world. Companies that participate in the global marketplace, especially those looking to tap into the BRIC economies, will do well to pay heed to the important lessons the rough diamonds can impart.

RETHINK THE RULES OF THE GAME

The rules of the business game have myriad applications. They can reward best practices and punish mistakes with brutal efficiency, whether through formal or informal sanctions. They define who participates in a particular market and to what extent. But the rules are never static, and up-and-coming entrants into the global economy continue to change the game. After all, if a continuous stream of rough diamonds is redefining the contours of global and BRIC competition, then we need to understand not only the rules as they exist today but the ways in which rough diamonds will transform the game going forward.

First and foremost, rough diamonds provide the undercurrent of dynamic global competition. Not only do they add growth and development, they also spawn new business models and successful practice. As Schumpeter suggested it would, creative destruction allows strong new companies to extend their advantages in emerging markets. This will not happen simply with a low-cost strategy, as conventional wisdom suggests, but through rigorous strategies focused on differentiation, innovation, and cost. Frankly, we should all know this lesson by now. Historically, when emerging firms move out from the shadow of the incumbent market leaders, they often do so on the strength of nontraditional strategies. Few people would have imagined that Samsung or Hyundai, once viewed as peripheral to high-quality brands, would now dominate the global market with highly attractive features and world-class innovation. Yet that's exactly what those companies have done.

The rough diamonds in this study share similar aspirations to the Japanese and Korean leaders today. Like the Samsungs and Hyundais of the world, the rough diamonds do not view themselves as purely low-cost providers for the global marketplace. While some of these firms might fill the low-cost position now, all of them aspire to design and provide high-quality products in the future. They have forged strategic partnerships with top multinational firms, universities, and business and research institutions around the world.

In our interviews, the rough diamond leaders have consistently reaffirmed their commitment to a steep learning trajectory—one that will enable them to lead global markets in the future. That starts with continuous learning and improvement, a development strategy the rough diamonds have already set in motion. How those efforts progress could well determine whether they become internationally recognized brands.

LOCAL IS THE NEW NORMAL

Local markets serve as the breeding grounds for current and future strategies. All too often, companies place too much emphasis on building scale and reaching a global scope. It's an understandable goal, given that a wider global footprint typically links with greater levels of product and process replication and lower per-unit costs. But the popular mantra of "going global" can distract from the fundamental improvements these companies can make at home. As we have seen with the rough diamonds, focusing on local priorities and interests can help companies discover untapped market niches by building scale through a more reasoned international strategy. For global strategists, it's not a question of global or local but the integration of both.

This integration has given rise to the term *glocal*, but catchphrases and hot new strategies don't lead to sustained, profitable growth. While many companies take a kneejerk approach to local markets, stripping down their products to lower costs for a developing market, these strategies have little chance of succeeding over the long haul. Major multinationals are not immune to this mistake. AT&T stumbled in China because it tried to build demand and did not recognize that many Chinese consumers bought phones to rent to other consumers.[1] Walmart, Google, and General Motors experienced challenges because they either underestimated or misinterpreted consumer response to their products.

Clearly there are some best practices by leading-edge Western businesses that others should benchmark and adopt, but their uncritical application with little regard for underlying local institutions and cultural mores will almost always limit results. Many multinational firms have successfully penetrated emerging markets, but studies prove that their success is inextricably tied to their ability to accommodate the intricate demands and preferences of the local market.[2]

What makes the local dynamics so vital in strategic and marketing decisions is that these markets are constantly evolving. The growth of the middle class, favorable government policies, and industry change continuously transform market segments and create opportunities for firms that take the time to understand local puts and takes. Domestic firms start with an advantage: their close proximity to and deep knowledge about the customers they're serving. They understand unfilled consumer demand and consumption patterns, and they typically can react to changes faster than companies watching from a distance. Rough diamonds are particularly adept at this. Russia's Velkom, China's Beingmate, Brazil's Açotubo, and India's Titan discerned nascent market niches and, in some cases, built a market presence even before these segments flourished into viable segments that outsiders noticed.

Even so, these advantages are not preordained. Multinational firms have their own unique capabilities for strengthening their presence in the local marketplace, but they need a proactive strategy to do so. Some progressive companies have found success by transforming their products in anticipation of undeveloped demands, as opposed to offering incremental changes in hopes of catching up with a market that's already moving in a new direction. Procter & Gamble captured the Chinese market in toothpaste by reformulating its product to accommodate a local preference for herbal elements and whiter teeth.[3] Coca-Cola transformed its distribution channel in Russia by acquiring the local company Multon and immediately widening its market presence in juices.

Top multinationals have often found considerable success with investments in the lives and well-being of consumers. Some have focused on building local workforces and empowering them to define local marketing activities. Procter & Gamble has done this in emerging markets around the world, and its management training programs have become a key draw for young managers in those countries.[4] Nike was able to solidify manufacturing operations for its sports hardware in Vietnam after working with surrounding local communities to assess and accommodate their needs.

REDUCE ETHNOCENTRIC TENDENCIES

Too often companies that are moving into new markets put too much stock in the superiority of their own business models and practices. Business scholars borrowed a word from their sociology brethren to describe this approach: *ethnocentricity*.[5] Two factors impel this misguided approach. First, companies that have great success with a strategy in a developed or other markets might believe it can be replicated with a few tweaks. Second, business leaders often believe emerging markets will evolve in the same manner as they did in more established economies. The combination leaves many companies trying to apply an existing strategy with a few minor, localized changes.

Managers have to make a concerted effort to counteract their natural ethnocentrism. They cannot eliminate it entirely, but they can recognize it exists and develop the necessary mechanisms to offset its undue influence.[6] One approach is adopting a reflexive mind-set that takes into account the nuances of the local culture and how they're reflected throughout society and the market.[7] The sustained success of rough diamonds rests in no small part on this type of reflexivity. Our research turned up numerous examples of firms that have creatively integrated Western management skills and business philosophies, such as supply chain innovations and supportive management systems, into strategies derived from their own cultural traditions, including creative application of relationships and strong family connections. The rough diamonds' ability to nurture cost and differentiation advantages did not develop in a vacuum; it incorporated strong considerations of local culture. The Chinese rough diamonds built relationships. Their counterparts in Brazil focused on their local brand legacies. The firms in Russia tapped into the home-grown managerial skills. And India's rough diamonds tapped into their country's indigenous talent.

These advantages grow out of a fertile seedbed of cultural traditions, historical legacies, and local innovations. These experiences don't always break favorably for domestic firms. For example, companies that have expanded beyond their local markets have often run into conflicts with the new consumers they touch. But on the whole, this local flavor plays a prominent role in business, commerce, and the sustained growth the rough diamonds have posted. It emanates from Brazil's deep pride in its ability to produce some of the world's best soccer players. It bubbles up from the energetic beat of the bossa nova and samba. In Russia and India, a rich history of indigenous technological know-how has produced an impressive legacy of scholars, artists, musicians, and scientists. While in the West, these factors are often treated as peripheral and secondary explanations for market tendencies, our study proved these sorts of influences often played a central role in rough diamond strategies.

RECOGNIZE THAT SOME CONVENTIONAL BELIEFS ABOUT EMERGING MARKETS NO LONGER APPLY

It's high time that firms from developed countries rethink their underlying conceptions about emerging markets. While these markets entice companies with their market size and potential, many companies are hesitant to tackle the myriad challenges, including underdeveloped institutions, inadequate governance, the lack of transparency, muddled market incentives, and the absence of accessible distribution channels.[8] These challenges have chased away many companies entirely. And for those that moved in anyway, these barriers often force them to fundamentally alter the business models that had worked so effectively in their more established markets.[9]

Because many key institutions remain underdeveloped in the BRIC countries, companies can easily generalize the challenges and not recognize the considerable advantages that lie just below the surface. Rather than take a passive and reactive approach to this lack of development, the rough diamonds use it as a source of motivation and urgency. While formal theories of development probably cannot account for intangibles such as these, our extensive interviews with a number of rough diamonds consistently revealed a drive to succeed that was integral to driving their strategies. The rough diamonds take an underdog mentality toward these institutional barriers—a key factor in their success, our research suggests. So while it might be hard to replicate that mind-set in a multinational firm, managers of virtually any company can work hard to instill the kind of entrepreneurial drive that sees the opportunities amid the challenges.

DEVELOP A CONTINGENCY PLAN FOR STRATEGIC PARTNERSHIPS WITH ROUGH DIAMONDS

The rough diamonds might well be formidable competitors, but they can also be strategic partners. The companies that disregard or undermine these rough diamonds might find themselves vulnerable should they come into direct competition. Understanding their motivations and aspirations can easily set the stage for important partnerships or supplier relationships in the future.

Harvard University marketing guru Clayton Christensen's book *The Innovator's Dilemma* is fast becoming a classic.[10] In his case-based research, Christensen argues that incumbent market leaders lose their leadership positions not because of poor management, but because they listened too intently to their lead consumers and were blindsided by the up-and-coming technologies and companies that eventually dislodged them. These disruptive technologies often started out as inferior options to existing products and services—even inferior to many of the ideas proposed by lead customers. But these same products quietly developed into prime-time disruptions.

The same holds true for the relationships between major multinationals and companies like the rough diamonds. Because these up-and-coming firms hone their businesses in relative obscurity, market leaders can find themselves blindsided because they do not anticipate the new trends or the new challengers that are shaping those trends. Some of the rough diamonds will have a consequential and disruptive impact on the future of the BRIC marketplaces and economies. It behooves firms in developed countries to take them seriously and prepare diligently for them, whether they're destined to become fierce competitors or key strategic partners.

CURRENT AND FUTURE ROUGH DIAMONDS SIGNAL THE SUSTAINED GROWTH OF EMERGING MARKETS

How long can emerging markets sustain these significant growth rates? Conventional analyses emphasize extrapolations from historical performance or focus on the institutional deficiencies as a drag on future expansion. Our study offers a new view: we consider the sustained growth as a generative process, fueled by the power of the existing and future rough diamonds. These markets will continue to produce an array of exemplary firms that sustain profitable growth over the long term. Of this we're certain.

So while the preoccupation of high growth alone can lead to a growth fetish, our view of sustainable growth in emerging markets addresses a different question: What traditions, opportunities, and skills inherent in emerging markets will enable succeeding generations of breakout firms? The case studies in this book describe many of the processes and growth strategies that rough diamonds adopt. But these anecdotes also provide a glimpse into the fundamental dynamics that have shaped, and will continue to shape, these exemplary firms.

Ultimately we hope the Four Cs can be as prescriptive as they are descriptive. We hope this for the major multinationals looking to build better businesses in the BRIC countries. We hope this as well for the soon-to-be rough diamonds, which would do well to observe the rise of the current group and replicate some elements of their developmental strategies.

We readily admit that by focusing on successful companies, this study has a highly optimistic tone. In fact, we are highly optimistic about these companies and these markets. These rough diamonds succeeded in difficult environments, often by pursuing strategies and systems that did not conform to more typical conceptions and practices in their local markets and around the rest of world. That makes the performance of these companies all the more impressive.

These different experiences throughout the four BRIC countries foreshadow the continuing emergence of a new set of rules for the business game. This transformation will inevitably influence the way companies conduct business throughout the global marketplace. The companies that embrace their impact and integrate it into their future strategies will thrive—and they will enjoy the sustained profitable growth that makes rough diamonds so valuable (box 10.1).

Box 10.1 Afterthoughts: A Preliminary Agenda

Suggestions	Implications for Your Business	Proposed Action Items
Rethink the rules of the game.	New competitors, notably rough diamonds, can bring new business models that can be disruptive.	Study key trends in emerging markets. Identify and map new competitors. Reexamine key assumptions about competition. Develop scenarios for addressing uncertainty.
Local is the new normal.	Competitive advantages will derive more from an understanding of the local market than an unqualified application of existing business models.	Establish a presence in targeted local markets. Hire as many locals to complement your expatriates. To the extent possible, delegate authority to local employees. Constantly reassess your methods for identifying future market needs and consumer consumption patterns in terms of targeted local markets.

(continued)

Suggestions	Implications for Your Business	Proposed Action Items
Reduce ethnocentric tendencies.	While there is merit in subscribing to best practice, most of these benchmarks are based on the experiences of successful firms from or operating in developed economies.	Adopt reflexivity in strategic planning: How might other cultures interpret our intent and actions? Seek advice and counsel from knowledgeable local authorities. Continue to question existing beliefs and assumptions.
Recognize that some conventional beliefs might no longer apply.	In this study, some accepted beliefs about emerging markets have been overturned and used by rough diamonds to their advantage.	Review core beliefs and assumptions. Study how new firms use institutional weaknesses to their advantage. Develop an institutional map of your targeted markets.
Plan for strategic partnerships.	New firms, such as rough diamonds, can be future competitors or partners.	Assess your complementary needs and assets against new business firms. Plan for partnerships (i.e., joint ventures) or competition (ways of achieving advantages that offset competitor actions) — or both.

Suggestions	Implications for Your Business	Proposed Action Items
Appreciate the importance of new exemplary firms in matters of sustainability in emerging markets.	Sustained growth in emerging markets might be better interpreted in the context of new breakout firms.	Reassess historical projections relating to the sustainability of emerging markets. Calibrate existing and future plans against the actual new firms, and not on projections alone.

Appendix: Methodology

W e agree with the scholars and practitioners who routinely find that performance is multidimensional.[1] And since it would be misleading to judge a firm's performance by focusing on a single measure, we considered multiple ways of evaluating company performances in emerging markets. After analyzing the defining characteristics of emerging markets, we settled on this set of performance measures and corresponding metrics:

- *Growth.* In the past several years, emerging markets have outpaced more established economies in terms of rate of growth. The gross domestic product growth rate of advanced markets during the recession in 2009 was −3.16 percent, which stands in sharp contrast to emerging markets that grew at 2.39 percent during the same time.[2] Many emerging market companies, such as Tata and Infosys in India, Cosco and Huawei in China, Severstal and Sistema in Russia, and Embraer in Brazil, have been lauded in academic journals and business publications for their impressive growth statistics. The rough diamonds also posted significant growth rates.

- *Market share.* While growth might be a good indicator of a company's potential, market share often can reflect a firm's dominance and its competitive advantage. As previous studies have outlined, strong market share is often associated with high profitability, such as the PIMS (Profit Impact of Market Strategy) Study.[3] Firms with high market share often enjoy competitive advantages because of their ability to set prices and influence relationships with suppliers, buyers, and other value chain members. In many cases, they also can mitigate their exposure to risk by controlling capacity utilization and passing cost fluctuations to suppliers and customers. Meanwhile, buyers tend to look at companies with high market share as having superior quality, even when they are not adequately informed about the brand.[4]

- *Profitability.* It is important for a firm in any market to meet profit goals. Profitability measures, especially return on assets and profit margin, validate the soundness and effectiveness of a firm's strategy. They commonly appear in financial reports and investor analyses, offer key indicators of managerial performance, and effectively help in evaluating shareholder returns. Over time, profitability can be more important for firms in emerging markets than for those in established markets. In the emerging markets, it serves as the core engine for driving future growth and development. Developed economies have formidable equity markets to rely on, while firms in emerging markets must look more heavily to internal resources for needed capital.

- *Efficiency.* Compared with companies in developed economies, firms in emerging markets often do not efficiently use their resources. Products sold in maturing markets typically assume a commodity status, which enables market leaders to base their business strategies on mass consumption. Many firms often use market demand for established products as a guide for decisions about growth and diversification. And when company leaders see stable demand for their products, they often do not work to develop new items or services. As a result, many firms in emerging markets can be viewed as less than innovative. In addition, they sometimes are seen as having weaker managers compared to their counterparts in developed countries. We define *efficiency* as a balanced allocation of resources. For example, to be successful, firms in any market must balance investments in new products with maintaining and producing current ones. In highly volatile emerging markets, efficiency is an especially important differentiator between potentially high-performing firms and disappointing ones.

To evaluate firm efficiency in the study, we used frontier analysis, a rigorous quantitative technique for comparing the alternative uses of resources relative to a predetermined standard (box A.1).

In adopting DEA to calculate efficiency scores, we selected two variables that we believe are the essential inputs in most economic models: the number of employees and registered capital. In addition, we chose output variables that capture the three aspects of performance we mentioned earlier: sales growth, market share, and profit margin. Collectively, output variables are defined as follows:

- *Sales growth:* Change in sales over the period, expressed in a percentage as the difference between last period's sales and this period's sales
- *Market share:* A firm's sales revenue in the product market divided by the total sales revenue in that market
- *Profitability:* Return on assets, defined as the ratio of net operating profit to the firm's start-of-year assets
- *Profit margin:* The ratio of net operating profit to sales

Box A.1 Frontier Analysis

Frontier analysis is a method used to understand the efficiency of decision-making units (DMUs): any unit with inputs and outputs, such as a production line or an entire firm. The efficiency of a DMU is determined by comparing the difference between the maximum outputs achievable given the set of inputs, so the DMU measures both optimal outputs and the minimum inputs required to reach a certain level of production.

Data envelopment analysis (DEA) is one simple form of frontier analysis that uses nonparametric linear programming to estimate the optimal input-output function (i.e., maximizes outputs or minimizes inputs). DEA has these underlying tenets:

- No assumption about input-output function
- No limits to the number of inputs and outputs
- Provides reference sets for benchmarking
- Provides useful information for input-output mix decision

Sources: T. J. Coelli, D.S.P. Rao, C. J. O'Donnell, and G. E. Battese, *An Introduction to Efficiency and Productivity Analysis*, 2nd ed. (New York: Springer, 2005). See also G. S. Yip, T. M. Devinney, and G. Johnson, "Measuring Long-Term Superior Performance: The UK's Long-Term Superior Performers, 1984–2003," *Long Range Planning* 42 (2009): 390–413.

CRITERIA SELECTION FOR IDENTIFYING THE ROUGH DIAMONDS

Applying these performance measures, we developed an exacting set of selection criteria for the rough diamonds:

1. The firm should be a privately owned company in the manufacturing sector with at least ten years of history.

2. The firm should be included in the 2009 Top 500 largest private companies list in their countries.

3. The firm's ten-year average of efficiency score (as determined by the frontier analysis) should be higher than the average of the annual Top 500 firms during the same period.

4. Its ten-year average sales growth rate should be higher than the average of the Top 500 firms.

5. Its ten-year average profitability should be higher than the average of the Top 500 firms.

6. Annual sales growth rate should not be lower than the Top 500 yearly average for more than three years.

7. The firm should be one of the top ten private companies in terms of sales in each market sector, defined by its four-digit Standard Industrial Classification (SIC) code in 2009.

8. Not more than two companies are selected from the same sector to avoid industry effects.

Using these criteria, we followed a comprehensive process of data collection to refine our selection of rough diamonds (box A.2).

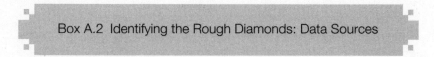

Box A.2 Identifying the Rough Diamonds: Data Sources

Quantitative Data Sources

The first step was to determine appropriate data sources to use. We selected China, Russia, Brazil, and India because they are among the largest emerging markets in the world. These countries have undergone rapid economic growth in recent decades and have the legacy of state ownership in their economies. We selected manufacturing industries because they are regarded as the generative engines of the economy in emerging markets.

We then focused on the Top 500 private firms in each year. For Chinese firms, we identified a list of the Top 500 firms by sales value each year from 2000 to 2009. For Russian and Indian firms, we identified a similar list each year from 2001 to 2009. For Brazilian firms, the time period is from 2003 to 2009 due to data availability. Our objective was to determine the best performers among the Top 500 firms across the years. Although not all large firms are high performers, we believe the best performers are among the larger ones. Because high performers have the ability to grow continuously, they eventually rank among the Top 500 firms over a given time period.

The data for Chinese firms come mainly from the Database of Industrial Firms in China, an annual industrial firm census conducted by China's National Bureau of Statistics (NBS). The *China Statistical Yearbook* offers aggregate statistics at the provincial and industry levels. The census data include all manufacturing enterprises except small, often family-run businesses at the village level. The annual survey database contains key financial indicators and demographic information, including the firm's name, manager's name, and year of establishment. The NBS reports that the accuracy of the information in the census, and in particular the financial data, has been carefully checked.

The data for Russia and Brazilian firms were obtained from ORBIS, a global database that has information on more than 60 million companies. The information is sourced from more than forty information providers, all experts in their regions or disciplines. As well as descriptive information and the company financials, ORBIS contains other details such as news, market research, ratings and country reports, scanned reports, ownership, and data on mergers and acquisitions. Raw data reports are available for listed companies, banks, and insurance companies, as well as major private firms.

The data for Indian firms were obtained from CMIE (Prowess). The coverage in Prowess of Indian firms is significant: it covers a fairly large proportion of the business conducted in India. For example, the total income of all companies in the Prowess database is about 78 percent of India's GDP. The output value of all the manufacturing companies included in Prowess accounted for 79 percent of the total output value for the country's entire registered manufacturing sector during 2008–2009. Prowess companies cover more than half of India's external trade and about 62 percent of India's exports and nearly 82 percent of its imports.

TABLE A.1 Comparison Firms

Name	Industry	Average Efficiency	Average Growth	Average Profit	Market Rank
China					
Jiangxi Zhengbang	Agriculture and animal husbandry	0.19	31.05%	2.59%	2
Shuanghui Group	Manufacturing of meat products	0.39	25.25%	6.32%	1
Guanxing Textile	Textile	0.19	35.15%	3.96%	4
Shanxi Lubao Group	Coking	0.27	44.74%	6.90%	5
Guizhou Xiyang Fertilizer	Chemical fertilizer	0.22	34.79%	8.29%	5
Liaoning Houying Group	Refractory materials	0.37	39.22%	12.47%	2
Holley Metering Limited	Energy meters	0.18	4.30%	3.88%	2
Russia					
Klinsky	Sausages and other prepared meat	0.30	15.67%	9.57%	8
Starodvorskie Kolbasy	Sausages and other prepared meat	0.36	33.67%	10.97%	6
Interagrosistemy	Canned fruits and vegetables	0.32	31.72%	10.61%	4
Pushkinskaya Ploshchad	Publishing and printing	0.24	13.23%	−12.40%	2
Kupol	Telephone and telegraph apparatus	0.41	−31.80%	17.97%	3
Ruiz Diamonds	Jewelry, precious metals	0.08	−7.00%	0.99%	2

(continued)

TABLE A.1 *(Continued)*

Name	Industry	Average Efficiency	Average Growth	Average Profit	Market Rank
India					
Godrej Industries	Industrial organic chemicals	0.31	2.69%	15.31%	4
Sona Koyo Steering Systems	Automobile ancillaries	0.22	9.24%	6.01%	7
Manakia	Aluminum and aluminum products	0.34	28.11%	7.81%	2
JK Lakshmi Cement	Cement	0.33	9.59%	17.88%	7
Kirloskar Ferrous	Pig iron	0.47	15.91%	10.40%	3
Kirloskar Electric	Electronic coils and transformers	0.23	42.93%	1.71%	4
Brazil					
Conservas Oderich	Canned fruits and vegetables	0.21	−8.00%	1.47%	2
Restoque	Women's footwear, except athletic	0.33	30.58%	13.09%	3
Holcim	Cement	0.18	26.67%	−12.96%	5
Apolo Tubos e Equipamentos	Steel pipe and tubes	0.42	33.49%	−5.74%	3
Mabe Campinas Eletrodomesticos	Household cooking equipment	0.46	3.22%	−5.83%	2

TABLE A.2 Top Twenty-Five Manufacturing Firms in BRIC, the United States, and the Rest of the World

Company Name	Core U.S. SIC, Text Description	Company Name	Core U.S. SIC, Text Description
China		**Russia**	
SAIC Motor	Motor vehicles and motor vehicle equipment	Federal Hydrogeneration Co. – RUSHYDRO	Electric transmission and distribution equipment
Baoshan Iron & Steel	Iron and steel foundries	OAO Severstal	Steel works, blast furnaces, and rolling and finishing
China FAW group	Motor vehicles and motor vehicle equipment	Novolipetskii Metallurgicheskii Kombinat – NLMK	Iron and steel foundries
Dongfeng Motor Group	Motor vehicles and motor vehicle equipment	Mechel OAO	Steel works, blast furnaces, and rolling and finishing
Aluminum Corporation of China	Rolling, drawing, and extruding of nonferrous metals	Magnitogorsk Iron & Steel Works – MMK	Iron and steel foundries
Hebei Iron & Steel	Primary smelting and refining of nonferrous metals	Lukoil-Nizhegorodnefteorgsintez	Miscellaneous products of petroleum and coal
Huawei Technologies.	Communications equipment	OAO TMK	Steel works, blast furnaces, and rolling and finishing
FAW-Volkswagen	Motor vehicles and motor vehicle equipment	Mosenergosbyt	Electric transmission and distribution equipment
Hongfujin Precision Industry (Shenzhen)	Computer and office equipment	Sibur Holding (closed joint stock company)	Miscellaneous products of petroleum and coal

(continued)

TABLE A.2 *(Continued)*

Company Name	Core U.S. SIC, Text Description	Company Name	Core U.S. SIC, Text Description
China		**Russia**	
Tech-Com (Shanghai) Computer	Computer and office equipment	LLC Lukoil PermnefteorgsinteZ	Miscellaneous products of petroleum and coal
Angang Steel Company	Iron and steel foundries	AVTOVAZ	Motor vehicles and motor vehicle equipment
Shanxi Taigang Stainless Steel	Steel works, blast furnaces, and rolling and finishing	OOO Lukoil-Volgogradneftepererabotka	Miscellaneous products of petroleum and coal
Nokia Telecommunications	Communications equipment	Federalnaya Setevaya Kompaniya Edinoi Energeticheskoi Sistemy	Electric transmission and distribution equipment
Shanghai General Motors	Motor vehicles and motor vehicle equipment	OAO Vyksunskii Metallurgicheskii Zavod	Steel works, blast furnaces, and rolling and finishing
Anshan Iron and Steel Group	Steel works, blast furnaces, and rolling and finishing	Moskovskaya Oblastnaya Elektrosetevaya Kompaniya	Electric transmission and distribution equipment
Wuhan Iron & Steel	Iron and steel foundries	Volkswagen Group Rus (limited liability company)	Motor vehicles and motor vehicle equipment
ZTE	Communications equipment	Chelyabinsk Metallurgical Plant OAO	Steel works, blast furnaces, and rolling and finishing
Compal Information Technology (Kunshan)	Computer and office equipment	Zapadno-Sibirskii Metallurgicheskii Kombinat	Steel works, blast furnaces, and rolling and finishing

Company	Industry	Company	Industry
Shanghai Volkswagen Automotive	Motor vehicles and motor vehicle equipment	Moscow Integrated Power (open joint stock company)	Electric transmission and distribution equipment
Shanghai Electric Group	Miscellaneous electrical machinery, equipment, and supplies	Protek OAO	Drugs
Maanshan Iron & Steel	Iron and steel foundries	Otkrytoe Aktsionernoe Obschestvo Gaz	Miscellaneous transportation equipment
Futaihua Industrial (Shenzhen)	Communications equipment	Taif-NK (public stock company)	Miscellaneous products of petroleum and coal
CNOOC Oil & Petrochemicals	Petroleum refining	SIA International	Drugs
Wuxi Huada Petrochemical Equipment	Special industry machinery, except metalworking machinery	OJSC Inter RAO UES	Electric transmission and distribution equipment
China National Heavy Duty Truck Group	Motor vehicles and motor vehicle equipment	Wimm-Bill-Dann Foods OJSC	Dairy products
India		**Brazil**	
Indian Oil	Miscellaneous products of petroleum and coal	JBS	Meat products
Reliance Industries	Plastics materials and synthetic resins, synthetic rubber, cellulosic, and other manmade fibers, except glass	Atlas Copco Brasil	General industrial machinery and equipment

(continued)

TABLE A.2 (Continued)

Company Name	Core U.S. SIC, Text Description	Company Name	Core U.S. SIC, Text Description
India		**Brazil**	
Tata Motors	Motor vehicles and motor vehicle equipment	Metalurgica Gerdau	Steel works, blast furnaces, and rolling and finishing
Tata Steel	Steel works, blast furnaces, and rolling and finishing	Gerdau	Steel works, blast furnaces, and rolling and finishing
Hindalco Industries	Primary smelting and refining of nonferrous metals	Braskem	Petroleum refining
MMTC	Jewelry, silverware, and plated ware	Companhia De Bebidas Das Americas – Ambev	Beverages
Larsen & Toubro	Special industry machinery, except metalworking machinery	BRF Brasil Foods	Meat products
Steel Authority of India	Metal forgings and stampings	Fiat Automoveis	Motor vehicles and motor vehicle equipment
Bharat Heavy Electricals	General industrial machinery and equipment	Textiles Omnes	Miscellaneous textile goods
Mangalore Refinery & Petrochemicals	Petroleum refining	Brasil Modelos Automotiva	Men's and boys' suits, coats, and overcoats
Maruti Suzuki India	Motor vehicles and motor vehicle equipment	Marfrig Alimentos	Meat products

Company	Product	Company	Product
Mahindra & Mahindra	Motor vehicles and motor vehicle equipment	Bunge Alimentos	Fats and oils
Chennai Petroleum	Petroleum refining	Companhia Siderurgica Nacional	Steel works, blast furnaces, and rolling and finishing
Sterlite Industries (India)	Rolling, drawing, and extruding of nonferrous metals	Vicunha Siderurgia	Metal forgings and stampings
JSW Steel	Steel works, blast furnaces, and rolling and finishing	Bunge Alimentos	Fats and oils
ITC	Cigarettes	Cargill Agricola	Fats and oils
Hyundai Motor India	Motor vehicles and motor vehicle equipment	Arcelor Mittal Brasil	Steel works, blast furnaces, and rolling and finishing
Grasim Industries	Cement, hydraulic	Rubbermix	Fabricated rubber products, not elsewhere specified
Hindustan Unilever	Soap, detergents and cleaning preparations, perfumes, cosmetics, and other toiletries	Usinas Siderurgicas DE Minas Gerais — USIMINAS	Steel works, blast furnaces, and rolling and finishing
Hero Motocorp	Motorcycles, bicycles, and parts	Companhia Brasiliana De Energia	Electric transmission and distribution equipment
Hindustan Aeronautics	Aircraft and parts	Embraer — Empresa Brasileira de Aeronautica	Aircraft and parts

(continued)

TABLE A.2 *(Continued)*

Company Name	Core U.S. SIC, Text Description	Company Name	Core U.S. SIC, Text Description
India		**Brazil**	
Aditya Birla Nuvo	Yarn and thread mills	Companhia Siderurgica Nacional	Steel works, blast furnaces, and rolling and finishing
Videocon Industries	Household appliances	BRF – Brasil Foods	Meat products
Jindal Steel & Power	Iron and steel foundries	Nestle Brasil	Dairy products
HCL Infosystems	Computer and office equipment	Volkswagen do Brasil Industria de Veiculos Automotores	Motor vehicles and motor vehicle equipment
United States		**World**	
Exxon Mobil	Petroleum refining	Exxon Mobil	Petroleum refining
Chevron	Petroleum refining	BP P.L.C.	Petroleum refining
Conocophillips	Petroleum refining	Chevron	Petroleum refining
General Motors	Motor vehicles and motor vehicle equipment	Conocophillips	Petroleum refining
Ford Motor	Motor vehicles and motor vehicle equipment	Toyota Motor	Motor vehicles and motor vehicle equipment
Hewlett-Packard	Computer and office equipment	Volkswagen	Motor vehicles and motor vehicle equipment
Valero Energy	Petroleum refining	General Motors	Motor vehicles and motor vehicle equipment
Apple	Computer and office equipment	Sabag Biel/Bienne	Millwork, veneer, plywood, and structural wood members

Company	Product	Company	Product
BP America	Petroleum refining	Samsung Electronics	Electronic components and accessories
Procter & Gamble	Soap, detergents and cleaning preparations, perfumes, cosmetics, and other toiletries	Daimler	Motor vehicles and motor vehicle equipment
Archer-Daniels-Midland	Grain mill products	Ford	Motor vehicles and motor vehicle equipment
Marathon Petroleum	Petroleum refining	Hewlett-Packard	Computer and office equipment
Philip Morris International	Cigarettes	Hitachi	Electrical industrial apparatus
Boeing	Aircraft and parts	Honda	Motorcycles, bicycles, and parts
Pfizer	Drugs	Nissan	Motor vehicles and motor vehicle equipment
Pepsico	Beverages	Panasonic	Household appliances
Johnson & Johnson	Drugs	BP America	Petroleum refining
Dell	Computer and office equipment	Siemens	Laboratory apparatus and analytical, optical, measuring, and controlling instruments
Caterpillar	Construction, mining, and materials handling machinery and equipment	Nestlé	Miscellaneous food preparations and kindred products

(continued)

TABLE A.2 (Continued)

Company Name	Core U.S. SIC, Text Description	Company Name	Core U.S. SIC, Text Description
United States		**World**	
Dow Chemical	Plastics materials and synthetic resins, synthetic rubber, cellulosic and other man-made fibers, except glass	Pemex Refinacion	Petroleum refining
United Technologies	Aircraft and parts	Emerson Electric (Asia)	Metalworking machinery and equipment
Kraft Foods	Dairy products	Flextronics Manufacturing (H.K.)	Electronic components and accessories
Intel	Electronic components and accessories	L.G.	Miscellaneous chemical products
Lockheed Martin	Aircraft and parts	Abinsa	Miscellaneous primary metal products
Sisco Systems	Communications equipment	Porsche	Motor vehicles and motor vehicle equipment

Source: Bureau van Dijk, Orbis data set.

CHECKING ROUGH DIAMONDS AGAINST THE COMPARISON GROUPS

To ascertain how the rough diamonds would perform against their peers, many of them acknowledged market leaders in the same industry or market segment, we compared the rough diamonds against a group of comparison companies (table A.1). To ensure compatibility, the pool from which we selected our comparison group was obtained from the Top 500 List in 2009 in their countries. We selected all comparable firms, similar in size and age, within the same business as the rough diamonds, as determined by four-digit SIC codes. And we collected qualitative information on all the companies. This procedure provided appropriate guidance about the factors that explain the rough diamonds' performance.

As a final check, Ernst & Young verified and confirmed the financial information for the final selection of rough diamonds. In some, if not most, cases, financial and market indicators alone do not fully capture the value of managerial skills and talents that might otherwise be better revealed in continued interpersonal interaction, field assessments, and shared experiences. As a consequence, some prospective rough diamonds were dropped, and a few were added on the strength of some qualitative factors. And with that we had our final list of rough diamonds.

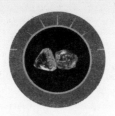

Notes

Chapter 1

1. See Shaomin Li and Seung Ho Park, "Guest Post: China's Mutant Turtles." *Financial Times*, August 3, 2011.
2. The Next Eleven (N-11) are eleven countries—Bangladesh, Egypt, Indonesia, Iran, Mexico, Nigeria, Pakistan, Philippines, South Korea, Turkey, and Vietnam; the CIVETS are Colombia, Indonesia, Vietnam, Egypt, Turkey, and South Africa; VISTA is an acronym for Vietnam, Indonesia, South Africa, Turkey, and Argentina.
3. See, in particular, Jim O'Neil, *The Growth Map: Economic Opportunity in the BRICs and Beyond* (New York: Portfolio/Penguin, 2011); and Ruchir Sharma, *Breakout Nations: In Pursuit of the Next Economic Miracles* (New York: Norton, 2012).
4. See Ernst & Young, *Rapid-Growth Markets Forecast, 2011*, 5.
5. See, in particular, Joseph Stiglitz, Amartya Sen, and Jean-Paul Fitoussi, *Mismeasuring Our Lives: Why GDP Doesn't Add Up* (New York: New Press, 2010).

Chapter 2

1. In this book, "late development" is the period following the initial industrialization that led to growth within the BRICs in the 2000s. In regard to RDs, late development thus describes the time of their rapid growth (2000–2010) rather than the date of their founding. The use of this time period is discussed further in chapter 3.
2. This adopts the perspective suggested by Henry Mintzberg, "Crafting Strategy," *Harvard Business Review* (July 1, 1987): 66–75.

Chapter 3

1. This is formally referred to as modernization theory. For a narrative, see Walt W. Rostow, *The Stages of Economic Growth: A Non-Communist Manifesto*, 2nd ed. (Cambridge, UK: Cambridge University Press, 1971).
2. Hira Group of Industries, "Group Companies," www.hiragroupindia.com /companies/gpil.php.
3. Obtained from the company's prospectus. See Formulário de Referência, 26.

Chapter 4

1. Industry fragmentation and consolidation are common themes in the strategy literature; see Michael E. Porter, *Competitive Strategy* (New York: Free Press, 1980). Demand aggregation refers to the pooling of energy sources or telecommunication services, or both, in developed countries. Even so, the lack of demand aggregation in developing economies in general was initially proposed by James Gollub, managing director of E-Cubed Enterprises in San Francisco.
2. For perspective on this issue, see M. B. Lieberman and D. B. Montgomery, "First Mover Advantages," *Strategic Management Journal* 9 (1998): 41–58.

Chapter 5

1. See Douglass C. North and Robert Paul Thomas, *The Rise of the Western World: A New Economic History* (Cambridge, UK: Cambridge University Press, 1973), 1–8.

Chapter 6

1. For a detailed discussion, see Joseph Boyett and Jimmie Boyett, *The Guru Guide to the Knowledge Economy: The Best Ideas for Operating Profitably in a Hyper-Competitive World* (Hoboken, NJ: Wiley, 2006), 105–106.
2. No causal association is claimed not only because the test itself is not designed to show causality, but because other intervening factors need to be considered. An alternative explanation is that the decisions about diversification tend to be broad and strategic in nature and should be conducted at the highest level of governmental and provincial bureaucracy instead of at the city or village levels.

Chapter 7

1. See Ernst & Young's *Rapid-Growth Markets Forecast, 2011.*
2. In this study, the average sales growth rate for the top 500 firms in BRIC is 26.80 percent per year for the past ten years. This means doubling the size of a firm at an astonishing rate of every 2.92 years.
3. Among the books that address this issue, see Akira Suehiro, *Catch-Up Industrialization: The Trajectory and Prospects of East Asian Economies* (Honolulu: University of Hawaii Press, 2008); Ian Bremmer, *Every Nation for Itself: Winners and Losers in a G-Zero World* (New York: Portfolio/Penguin,

2012); and Dambisa Moyo, *Winner Take All: China's Race for Resources and What It Means for the World* (New York: Perseus Books, 2012).

4. Tarun Khanna and Krishna Palepu, *Winning in Emergent Markets: A Roadmap for Strategy and Execution* (Boston: Harvard Business School Publishing, 2010).

5. World Commission on Environment and Development, *Our Common Future: Report of the World Commission on Environment and Development,* United Nations General Assembly Document A/42/427, August 2, 1987. Retrieved from www.un-documents.net/wced-ocf.htm.

6. This is oriented at outcomes as opposed to process. Studies of growth in developed markets also focus on entrepreneurial activities. In this study, however, our treatment of entrepreneurship is oriented more to the process of attaining growth than the end in itself.

7. See, for example, P. Farris, M. J. Moore, and R. Buzzell, *The Profit Impact of Marketing Strategy Project: Retrospect and Prospects* (Cambridge, UK: Cambridge University Press, 2004).

8. Jeffrey Madrick, *Why Economies Grow: The Forces That Shape Prosperity and How We Can Get Them to Work Again* (New York: Basic Books, 2002).

9. F. Knickerbocker, *Oligopolistic Reaction and Multinational Enterprises* (Cambridge, MA: Harvard University Press, 1973).

10. Farris, Moore, and Buzzell, *The Profit Impact of Marketing Strategy Project.*

11. See the review by J. Kimberly, "Organizational Size and Structuralist Perspective: A Review, Critique, and Proposal," *Administrative Science Quarterly* 21 (1979): 571–597.

12. The precedent for this table is the much acclaimed Boston Consulting Group growth matrix, in which the cells are classified as "Stars," "Cash Cows," "Questions Marks," and "Dogs," depending on market growth and relative market share.

13. Xiaobo Wu, *The Big Failures* (Hangzhou: Zhejiang People's Publishing House, 2000).

14. For a good discussion of cost leadership and product differentiation, see Michael E. Porter, *Competitive Strategy* (New York: Free Press, 1980).

15. Tarun Khanna and K. Palepu, "Why Focused Strategies May Be Wrong for Emerging Markets," *Harvard Business Review* 75 (1997): 41–51.

16. Ibid.

Chapter 8

1. Ministry of Statistics and Programme Implementation (Government of India, New Delhi), National Accounts Statistics, 2007–2008.

2. Rex A. Hudson, ed. *Brazil: A Country Study* (Washington, DC: GPO for the Library of Congress, 1997), http://countrystudies.us/brazil/78.htm. The number of privatizations under Cardoso is taken from Daniel Triesman, "Cardoso, Menem, and Machiavelli: Political Tactics and Privatization in Latin America," *Studies in Comparative International Development,* 38, no 3 (Fall 2003): 93–109.

3. Banco Central do Brasil, *Annual Report* (2009), www.bcb.gov.br/?AR2009.

4. For a narrative on these trends, see Uri Dadush and William Shaw, *Juggernaut: How Emerging Markets Are Reshaping Globalization* (Washington, DC: Carnegie Endowment for International Peace, 2011).

5. Michael E. Porter, *Competitive Strategy* (New York: Free Press, 1980).

6. Andrew Grove, *Only the Paranoid Survive: How to Exploit the Crisis Point That Challenges Every Company* (New York: Random House, 1999).

7. Porter, *Competitive Strategy.*

8. Wikiinvest, "Rise of China's Middle Class," www.wikinvest.com/concept /Rise_of_China's_Middle_Class.

9. See Ernst & Young, *Rapid-Growth Markets Forecast, 2011*, 16.

10. For a critique of GNP as a measure of progress, see Joseph Stiglitz, Amartya Sen, and Jean-Paul Fitoussi, *Mismeasuring Our Lives: Why GDP Doesn't Add Up* (New York: New Press, 2010). Similar arguments have been raised by Ha-Joon Chang, *Rethinking Development Economics* (London: Anthon Press, 2006), and by Herman Daly and John Cobb, *For the Common Good* (Boston: Beacon Press, 1994). However, it was development economist Sixto K. Roxas who had earlier distinguished between growth, development, and transformation in his master's thesis: "Change, Development, and Growth of Underdeveloped Economies" (Fordham University, 1954).

11. See J. A. Mathews, *Dragon Multinationals: A New Model of Global Growth* (New York: Oxford University Press, 2002); Jim Joseph, *The Experience Effect: Engage Your Consumers with a Consistent and Memorable Brand Experience* (New York: AMACOM, 2010); Yi Zhang, Zigang Zhang, and Zhixue Liu, "Choice of Entry Modes in Sequential FDIs in an Emerging Economy," *Management Decision* 45 (2007): 749–772.

Chapter 9

1. Thomas Gold, Douglas Guthrie, and David Wank, *Social Connections in China: Institutions, Culture and the Changing Nature of Guanxi* (Cambridge, UK: Cambridge University Press, 2002).

Chapter 10

1. Maria Flores Letelier, Fernando Flores, and Charles Spinosa, "Developing Productive Consumers in Emerging Markets," *California Management Review* 45, no. 4 (2003): 77–103. For other cases, see Seung Ho Park and Wilfried Vanhonacker, "The Challenge for Multinationals in China: Think Local, Act Global," *MIT Sloan Management Review* 48, no. 4 (2007): 48–54.

2. Satish Shankar, Charles Ormiston, Nicolas Bloch, Robert Schaus, and Vijay Vishwanath, "How to Win in Emerging Markets," *MIT Sloan Management Review* 49 (2008): 19–23.

3. These examples are cited in ibid.

4. Ibid., 22.

5. "William Graham Sumner," *Wikipedia*, http://en.wikipedia.org/wiki/William_Graham_Sumner.

6. Ken Barger. www.iupui.edu/~anthkb/ethnocen.htm.

7. See an excellent account by Richard Whittington, *What Is Strategy—and Does It Matter?* (New York: Routledge, 1993).

8. William Wilson and Nikolay Ushakov, "Brave New World Categorizing the Emerging Market Economies: A New Methodology," *SKOLKOVO Emerging Market Index* (February 2011). See also Khanna and Palepu, *Winning in Emergent Markets.*

9. See Park and Vanhonacker, "The Challenge for Multinationals in China."

10. Clayton Christensen, *The Innovator's Dilemma: When New Technologies Cause Great Firms to Fail* (Boston: Harvard Business School Press, 1997).

Appendix

1. Multiple and conflicting performance measures are widely acknowledged in business. For a sample of such narratives, see Robert C. Higgins, *Analysis for Financial Management*, 5th ed. (New York: McGraw-Hill, 1998), and Lawrence Revsine, Daniel Collins, and W. Bruce Johnson, *Financial Reporting and Analysis* (Upper Saddle River, NJ: Prentice Hall, 2001).

2. International Monetary Fund, *World Economic Outlook Database* (2010).

3. The findings discussed in this section are based on R. D. Buzzell and B. T. Gale, *The PIMS Principles: Linking Strategy to Performance* (New York: Free Press, 1987). In this work, it is reported that an increase of ten percentage points in market share is typically associated with an increase of five points of pretax return on investment. At present, this finding is considered to be far from conclusive because of the many criticisms directed at the PIMS methodology. For a perspective on this, see Robert D. Buzzell, "The PIMS Program of Strategy Research: A Retrospective Appraisal." *Journal of Business Research* 579, no. 1 (2004): 478–483.

4. See Roger J. Best, *Market-Based Management: Strategies for Growing Consumer Value and Profitability* (Upper Saddle River, NJ: Prentice Hall, 1997/2000).

The Authors

Seung Ho Park is the executive director of the Institute for Emerging Market Studies (IEMS) and the Chair Professor of Strategy at the Moscow School of Management SKOLKOVO. Prior to joining IEMS, he was the founding president of the Samsung Economic Research Institute in China, and the director of the Center for Emerging Market Strategy and BAT Chair Professor at the China Europe International Business School. He has also taught at several universities in the United States and Hong Kong, including Rutgers University, the University of Texas–Dallas, Hong Kong University of Science and Technology, and the City University of Hong Kong. His research focuses on market competition and the sustained growth of local and multinational companies in emerging markets. He can be reached at spark@skolkovo.ru.

Nan Zhou is an assistant professor at SKOLKOVO Business School and a research fellow at IEMS. Her research addresses questions that intersect the fields of corporate strategy and international business, focusing primarily on understanding

205

how strategic decisions such as product diversification and globalization are influenced by firm resources and institutional environments in the context of emerging markets. She can be reached at Nan_Zhou@skolkovo.ru.

Gerardo R. Ungson is a Non-Resident Senior Research Fellow at IEMS and the Y. F. Chang Endowed Chair Professor of International Business at the College of Business, San Francisco State University. He is the coauthor of six books on various topics, including global strategy, management, and Korean management systems. In addition to his work on emerging markets, he is engaged in poverty alleviation research in the Philippines. He can be reached at bungson@sfsu.edu.

Index

Page numbers in italics refer to tables and figures.